AN EXPERIMENT IN LIBERTY

AN EXPERIMENT IN LIBERTY

America's Path to Independence

George Grant

canonpress
Moscow, Idaho

Published by Canon Press
P.O. Box 8729, Moscow, Idaho 83843
800.488.2034 | www.canonpress.com

Second edition: 2022. First edition published by Standfast.

Cover design by James Engerbretson.
Interior design by Valerie Anne Bost.

Printed in the United States of America.

Some of this material originally appeared in *To Pledge Allegiance* (Powder Springs, GA:
American Vision, 2005).

Library of Congress Cataloging-in-Publication Data forthcoming

22 23 24 25 26 27 28 29   10 9 8 7 6 5 4 3 2 1

To my students and colleagues at Franklin Classical School,
and to my yokefellows at the King's Meadow Study Center

CONTENTS

INTRODUCTION

"Whatever makes a man a good Christian also makes him a good citizen."

DANIEL WEBSTER

G.K. Chesterton once quipped, "America is the only nation in the world that is founded on a creed." Other nations find their identity and cohesion in ethnicity, or geography, or partisan ideology, or cultural tradition, he argued. But America was founded on certain ideas—ideas about freedom, about human dignity, and about social responsibility.

It was this profound peculiarity that most struck Alexis de Tocqueville during his famous visit to this land at the beginning of the nineteenth century. He called it "American exceptionalism." At about the same time de Tocqueville penned his sage observations in *Democracy in America*, a number of educators in the fledgling republic began to realize that if their great experiment in liberty, their extraordinary American exceptionalism, were to be maintained over the course of succeeding generations, then an informed patriotism would have to be instilled in the hearts and minds of the young. Indeed, John Quincy Adams wrote, "Posterity: you will never know how much it has cost my generation to preserve your freedom. I hope you will make good use of it."

Thus, from the middle of the nineteenth century to the middle of the twentieth, rising citizens were presented with small handbooks—brief guides to the essential elements of the American creed. Pastors, statesmen, educators, and parents wanted to somehow pass on to posterity the moral and constitutional tools necessary to make good use of their freedom. A decade ago, after collecting a representative sample of such handbooks from dusty antiquarian bookshops, I put together *The Patriot's Handbook* as an updated summary of that vaunted tradition. It contained a concise introduction to the foundational ideas, documents, events, and personalities of American freedom. It is a citizenship primer for a whole new generation of American patriots.

But I always felt that I should provide a moral philosophy thread to tie those artifacts together into a coherent narrative; thus, this book.

Separating fact from fiction, exactitude from nostalgia, and actuality from myth in early American history is often more than a little difficult. Though it is perhaps unwise to have anything like an idealized perception of that great epoch, it is difficult to dismiss the breadth and depth of the fledgling colonial culture and the substantive character of the people who populated it. Living in a day when genuine heroes are few and far between—at best—those pioneers and the times they vivified provide a startling contrast.

The fact is, colonial America produced an extraordinary number of prodigiously gifted men. From William Byrd and George Wythe to Peyton Randolph and Patrick Henry, from Samuel Adams and John Hancock to Benjamin Franklin and George Washington, the legacy of the seventeenth-century's native-born geniuses remains unmatched. Their accomplishments—literary, scientific, economic, political, and cultural—are staggering to consider. According to historian Paul Johnson, "Never before has one place and one time given rise to so many great men."

There are very few things that modern historians can agree on. But when it comes to God and His heroes, there is sudden consensus. The long-held notion that history is His story is fiercely resisted in our day. The once dominant view that history is not merely the record of what happened in the past but that it is a kind of moral philosophy worked out by great men and women of vision has been replaced by the odd assertions and assumptions of a handful of experts. It is too easy for us to forget—or to try to ignore—the fact that the doings of man are on the knees of an inscrutable and sovereign God. It is too easy for us to forget that the record of the ages is actually philosophy teaching by example.

Because the past is ever present, giving shape and focus to all our lives, it is not what was, but whatever seems to have been, simply because the past, like the future, is part and parcel of the faith. In this volume, we try to remind ourselves of these important facts.

Alexis de Tocqueville has oft been quoted—perhaps apocryphally—saying:

> I sought for the greatness and genius of America in her commodious harbors and her ample rivers, and it was not there; in her fertile fields and

boundless prairies, and it was not there; in her rich mines and her vast world commerce, and it was not there. Not until I went to the churches of America and heard her pulpits aflame with righteousness did I understand the secret of her genius and power. America is great because she is good and if America ever ceases to be good, America will cease to be great.

This narrative survey is offered in the hope that the ideas that made America both great and good may once again become the common currency of our national life. It is offered in the hope that the secret of our genius and power might be broadcast far and wide—and essentially cease to be a secret.

CHAPTER 1: THE DIVERSE COLONIES

"Statesmen may plan and speculate for liberty, but it is Religion and Morality alone, which can establish the Principles upon which Freedom can securely stand."

JOHN ADAMS

America has often been described as the world's great "melting pot." People from the four corners of the earth came together on these shores in a common pursuit of freedom and opportunity, despite the wild diversity of their social, economic, ethnic, and cultural backgrounds. Eventually they would come from every nation, tongue, and tribe on earth, but even in the earliest days of the colonial settlements, very different peoples with very different perspectives and very different aspirations combined their strengths to create a new national character altogether unique in the annals of history. It was a character that would ultimately unite those very different peoples politically and culturally and usher in one of the greatest cultural flowerings the world has ever known.

GREAT DIVIDES

At first, deep divisions marked the character of the emerging colonies, reflecting divergent beliefs and practices. Many of the settlers had left their countries due to the religious conflicts that were then raging throughout Europe—particularly in Britain—during the 16th and 17th Centuries. The Protestant Reformation, which attempted to restore the old ideals of Christendom according to the pattern of the Bible, provoked a dramatic Roman Catholic Counter-Reformation. The resulting clash of kingdoms, institutions, and ambitions increased tensions across the Continent and unleashed terrible persecutions, purges, and pogroms. The social, cultural, and political tumult convinced many devout believers to flee to the New World where they hoped to find the peace and freedom necessary to realize their vision of a Holy Commonwealth.

Many others came to the New World for financial opportunities and social advancement. The rigid aristocracies that dominated virtually every country in Europe made social mobility for ordinary merchant and peasant classes very difficult, if not impossible. Even the old craft guilds and trade societies which had once paved the way for a Medieval middle class now made it difficult for young, energetic workers to enter into new businesses. The New World's vast, untapped resources and absence of a hierarchical social structure made it attractive to these hopeful entrepreneurs, who wanted to venture out, take risks, and enjoy the fruits of their labors on their own terms. Of course, not all of these opportunists came to the colonies with pure motives. A few, who had little or no grounding in Biblical standards of stewardship, were motivated only by their unquenchable desire for riches and status. As a result, conflicts and difficulties would arise in the colonies even in the earliest, halcyon days.

The shifting political tides of Europe also forced many settlers to the New World. Escalating political conflicts—caused by war, succession crises, economic pressure, and civil unrest—created waves of refugees. The English Civil War, fought between Parliament and King Charles I, divided Britain into factions: the Puritans, the Levelers, the Cavaliers, the Covenanters, and the Roundheads. Ultimately, Parliament won the war, executed Charles, and sent his supporters fleeing. But the return of the king's son, Charles II, to the English throne in 1660 soon sent waves of Parliamentary supporters to the shores of America. The conflict between Crown and Parliament would be replayed a few decades later during the Glorious Revolution of 1688, sending still more settlers across the Atlantic.

However, the political turmoil was not confined to Britain. In France, Roman Catholic monarchs squared off against the French Protestants, the Huguenots, and regularly put them to flight to havens throughout Europe, England, Ireland, and America. In the various German kingdoms, Protestant and Catholic fortunes teetered back and forth, unsettling families in search of peace and security. Likewise, the struggle for the ascendancy in the Hapsburg Dutch and Spanish realms displaced thousands and added to the stream of immigrants to the New World.

Some people came because of spiritual concerns. Some came because of economic or social ambitions. Others came to avoid the political disarray, heed the lure of adventure, or run from their sordid pasts. Still others simply followed friends and neighbors. Clearly, the people of the developing colonies came from a number of different cultures for a variety of reasons—some good, some bad. But they came. They arrived on the shores of the New World in droves. As the populations swelled, the individual qualities of each colony became more pronounced, and soon, the differences between the colonies were obvious to even the most casual observers. As communities spread up and down the eastern American seaboard, groups of colonies began to take on a distinctive regional flavor and further developed the cultural diversity that has marked the American existence ever since.

DIFFERENT HOPES
FOR DIFFERENT FOLKS

Of course, the circumstances leading to the establishment of the various colonies were as varied as the character they assumed while they continued to grow further into the American wilderness. Whether religion, profit, or politics served as the motive, immigrants moved and transplanted their cultures when they came. Colonies that started as small communities quickly became vast and diverse.

Virginia

Virginia, the first English colony to be established, was intended to create an economically viable and profitable market for investors back in London. Thus, while the Virginia Charter, granted by James I, expressed the intent to propagate the Christian religion, and while the first settlement, Jamestown, had many

Christian settlers, the primary motive for the colony was commercial, making it an essentially secular venture.

Because the settlement was a profit-driven venture, owned by businessmen back in England who were prominent members of the aristocracy, the leaders of the colony maintained firm political support for the Crown and the interests of the nobility. Accordingly, they fully embraced the established Church of England, maintained their allegiance to Charles I during the English Civil War, and resisted attempts to be governed by Parliament after the Puritan victory.

But the troubles back home distracted Parliamentary officials from the affairs across the ocean, and thus, the colony was able to operate with a fair degree of autonomy. The House of Burgesses, the first representative body in North America, became an active voice in the governance of the colony. Once Charles II returned to England and assumed his father's throne, the young king rewarded the Colonists' loyalty by attempting to limit their home rule, which set the stage for many confrontations between crown administrators and the House of Burgesses in the years to come.

The restoration of the Stewart dynasty also prompted many religious dissenters, particularly Baptists from England and Wales and Presbyterians from Scotland and Ireland, to eventually settle in the colony. Moreover, it was in Virginia that chattel slavery, the bane of American life for centuries afterward, was introduced—adding yet another dimension to the diversity of the settlement.

Massachusetts

The colonial settlements in New England were very different from that of Virginia. The colonization efforts there were primarily religious, with settlers coming to the New World to escape religious persecution in England. In what is known as the Great Migration, nearly 24,000 Puritans, many of them men of means, took to the seas, bound for New England from 1632-1640 in the largest departure from the Old World to any destination ever.

Whereas in Virginia the authorities had to ship in prospective wives in 1619 to add some stability to the venture, the settlement of Massachusetts was a family affair from the beginning. But while the Puritans that settled there were religious dissenters, they too were loyal to the crown. The leaders of the new colony formed the Massachusetts Bay Company and eventually secured a charter from King Charles on March 4, 1629. The charter spelled out that, unlike Virginia, this was to be a religious settlement, set apart for the purpose of preserving the religious liberties of those in opposition to the established Church of England. But since they landed in Cape Cod outside the boundaries of their original charter, they had to establish their own government. Initially, they elected their governors, as opposed to having them appointed by the king. The fact that the inhabitants were not part of the English aristocracy gave the Massachusetts Bay and Plymouth colonies an independent streak that would continue to play out as the colonies struggled for independence.

Rhode Island

The colonies in Massachusetts, founded for religious dissenters from the Church of England, soon had a new class of religious dissenters of its own. In January 1636, Roger Williams set out from Massachusetts with 20 supporters to found a new colony. Williams had run afoul of the Puritan leaders with his uncompromising, incendiary rhetoric, his radical demands for complete separation from all those he considered worldly, and his rejection of covenant theology and the corresponding contract theory which formed the basis for the Puritan community, its legal code, and its cultural impetus. This small group would found Rhode Island, with colonial settlements being established in Providence, Warwick, Portsmouth, and Newport.

The government system in Rhode Island was dedicated to drawing sharp distinctions between the spheres of the church and state, which eventually drew a large number of religious dissenters, radicals, and sects to the colony. The Baptists founded their first church in America at Rhode Island in 1639. The Quakers, who eventually became a political problem for Williams, came shortly afterward. Interestingly, despite the colony's extreme stance on religious tolerance, Rhode Island would become one of the primary chattel slave trading centers in New England, with slaves needed to farm the plantations and raise the livestock of the colony. Due to this burgeoning slave trade and the increasingly profitable trans-Atlantic commerce with England, shipbuilding became one of the leading industries in the small colony.

Connecticut

Connecticut was also established in 1636 when Thomas Hooker, a Puritan, left Massachusetts Bay with 100 supporters to settle the Connecticut River Valley. There they hoped to expand and extend the idea of the "holy commonweal," which they had come to believe was being compromised back in the bustling commercial center of Boston. Later, John Davenport arrived in Connecticut to found the New Haven colony, which he dedicated to establishing an even "purer" form of Puritanism. Charles II later granted a charter to John Winthrop, Jr., which would absorb both colonies under one administration. Puritans were also primary settlers in what became New Hampshire, which was declared a separate colony in 1679.

With the exception of Rhode Island, the entire region of New England was made up predominantly of Puritans who rejected the established Church of England. The churches, while Reformed in doctrine, adhered to the congregational system, which was later reflected in the participation of the citizens in their local assemblies. As religious dissenters, they readily claimed their religious and political rights when challenged by the crown, which would make the area a hotbed of resistance in the years leading up to the War of Independence. That climate of liberty and virtue became an open invitation to waves of like-minded Puritan settlers, who came to the region to flee the religious and political morass in England.

New York

The Mid-Atlantic colonies developed very differently than either the New England or the Virginia settlements. New Netherlands was first settled by Dutch traders and was little more than a fur trading post for several decades. Despite being founded by a Protestant nation with the established Dutch Reformed church, it was never a religious settlement. The English eventually took control of the colony in 1664. It was then granted by Charles II to his younger brother, the Duke of York—who later ascended the throne as James II. Thus, the settlement came to be known as New York Province.

Under James's personal administration, the Church of England became the established religion of the new possession; however, the settlers were not always happy with his rule. In the 1670s, they demanded a representative assembly, which was eventually granted. They quickly passed the Charter of Liberties and Privileges, which claimed their political and legal rights as British subjects. James, once crowned king, revoked the charter, but William and Mary would restore those rights in 1691, after James was sent into exile following the Glorious Revolution of 1688.

New Jersey

New Jersey also sprang from the original royal land grant to the Duke of York. Puritans from Long Island first settled it, but the western portion of the territory was sold to and inhabited by Quakers in 1674. The area grew divided by competing claims to the property, which prompted the crown to unite the divided colonies as the royal colony of New Jersey in 1702.

Pennsylvania

Across the Delaware River from New Jersey, the Quaker leader William Penn hoped to create a haven for the religious group and obtained a grant from Charles II to set up a colony as a "Holy Experiment" in 1681. Quakers were suffering persecution back in England, and even though Penn himself had spent time in prison for his religious beliefs, he secured the charter as a repayment by the king for debts owed to his father. Penn quickly began to organize the new colony on the basis of Quaker doctrine and the principles of religious liberty. Soon, the newly established city of Philadelphia became one of the busiest ports and economic centers in the New World.

But a stream of non-Quaker immigrants began to arrive from England and became the majority population base. German Lutherans and Anabaptists also settled further west on the frontier. When the pacifist beliefs of the Quakers' leaders made them reluctant to respond to threats from attacks on the colony by Indians and the French, a governmental crisis arose. New leaders began to emerge, including the young Benjamin Franklin. A defensive militia was organized and supplied to counter the threats, and the influence of the Quakers in the colony steadily declined as the population continued to swell.

Delaware

Delaware also emerged from the territory granted to Penn. Originally settled by Swedish Lutherans, the area later came into the hands of the Dutch. Less than a decade later, in 1682, the Dutch turned it over to the English, and Charles II sold it to Penn, who was just in the process of establishing Pennsylvania. However, the English settlers that arrived were not content with Quaker rule, and they increasingly called for independence from the Pennsylvania colony. With the three counties they occupied geographically isolated on the other side of the Delaware River, Penn granted their wish in 1704 and allowed a separate representative assembly to be elected under his supervision. This degree of independence made Delaware one of the strongest voices for liberty in the growing conflict with the English Empire.

Maryland

Just south of Penn's religious colony was Maryland, chartered in 1632. The proprietor, George Calvert, later Lord Baltimore, was a Roman Catholic convert who obtained the grant from Charles I in return for his support against Parliament in the time leading up to the English Civil War. Calvert intended to have the colony settled by Roman Catholic refugees, but most of the settlers turned out to be Protestants. This incongruity didn't deter George's son and successor, Cecilius Calvert, from attempting to build a colony dedicated to preserving peace between Christians of all backgrounds. This approach was helpful in diffusing tensions when Puritan and Baptists were expelled from the neighboring Virginia colony in 1643 and came to Maryland. Some of the Puritans settled Providence in 1649, which eventually was renamed and became the capital, Annapolis. Calvert also maintained his stance on religious liberties during the escalating hostilities between the Puritan Parliament and the Roman Catholic-leaning Charles I by adopting the Toleration Act in 1648, which granted religious freedom to all Christians.

In the following years, during the English Commonwealth and the Protectorate under Oliver Cromwell, Maryland became a haven for the King's supporters, known as Cavaliers. Despite the political troubles at home, the Calvert family continued to rule the colony for seven generations and it was the only proprietary colony still in operation when independence was declared in 1776.

South Carolina

Just south of Virginia was the vast colony of Carolina, which had not attracted settlers when a grant was issued in 1628. A wave of immigrants eventually arrived after 1650, but not from England; rather, inhabitants of the New World, from Virginia and New England, developed the colony. After Charles II was restored to the throne in 1660, he granted the land to his supporters, who in 1663 made promises of land grants and religious freedoms in the opening territory. Immigrants flooded the area such that, while the proprietors wanted an orderly settlement, there was nothing they could do to prevent new arrivals from pushing inward well into the frontier.

In 1664, a new wave of settlers arrived from Barbados, who established Cape Fear and brought a number of slaves with them. The slave trade would become firmly established in Carolina as the settlers turned to a new, labor-intensive cash crop: rice. The commerce that rice would produce made Charleston one of the fastest growing cities in the southern colonies.

North Carolina

In 1702, the Church of England was established in the colony, but that did not deter large groups of German and Swedish Lutheran immigrants from settling there—especially along the northern frontier. The contrast with the very urbane and English south was evident from the start. Eventually, growing tensions between the regions demanded that the vast colonial administration be divided in 1712, thus creating two separate colonies—North and South Carolina.

Georgia

The southern Carolina territory was divided again when the new colony of Georgia was settled in 1733 under the supervision of

General John Oglethorpe. The English administrators intended the colony to be a residence for the poor and needy from England. This peculiar plan caught the attention of many Christians, who supported the endeavor financially and eventually settled there. Georgia also attracted many Protestant refugees from Europe, including Germans, fleeing Hapsburg persecution, and avid Presbyterian Highlanders, fleeing English political oppression in Scotland. This distinctly Christian settlement in the south attracted a wide range of ministers and religious workers, including George Whitefield, who would help launch the Great Awakening in Georgia, and the Methodist pioneers John and Charles Wesley. The colony even attracted a contingent of Jewish refugees from Western and Central Europe, who eventually settled in Savannah.

Economic hardships in the colony prompted some significant changes to the colony in the following years. While Georgia prohibited slavery with the firm endorsement of General Oglethorpe, over time popular sentiments began to change, and in 1750, the colony began to allow slavery. Georgia would struggle with the slavery question for more than a hundred years afterward, with the clergy actively opposed to the practice.

MORE THAN JUST THE THIRTEEN

Besides these thirteen rather well-known colonies, a number of other fledgling settlements stretched out across the vast American frontier. Across the Appalachian Ridge in the South, the "over-mountain" settlers established the Wautaga Province—which would later become Tennessee—as early as 1723. The rugged Puritan pioneers of Western New Hampshire and Northern

New York established the colonial province of Vermont in 1724. Intrepid settlers from Georgia and South Carolina rounded Florida into the Gulf of Mexico and took over the old Spanish colonial outposts at Mobile, Pensacola, and Baton Rouge, establishing the West Florida province as early as 1755. And of course, the hardy, northern English trappers, traders, soldiers, and adventurers gained control of the five Canadian colonies beginning in 1763. Most of these more obscure colonies would eventually follow a common path of independence and still later find their destinies in union with the other, better known thirteen—Vermont in 1791, Watauga in 1799, and West Florida in 1810.

From the bustling trading ports of Boston, New York, Philadelphia, and Baltimore to the tobacco and rice farms of Virginia and the Carolinas, America's melting pot was brewing. The result was a unique colonial culture that combined elements of the New World with the Old World to create a civilization—and a political atmosphere—like none before or since.

SOMETHING OLD, SOMETHING NEW

The confluence of society, science, religion, and political climate in the colonies produced a culture unparalleled in the world. While the colonies still lacked any substantial social cohesiveness, the diverse mixture of old-world interests combined with a new-world talent and innovation resulted in an explosion of imagination and opportunity across the rapidly expanding American map. Freed from the lingering feudal constraints of class, nobility, and the European social order, and bringing skills and experience from their homelands, the citizens of the colonies began to experiment in a number of new and exciting ways.

One factor in making America such a productive center for innovation and invention was the pioneer spirit of adventure, combined with the uniquely English interest in scientific advancement. This created an almost insatiable appetite to discover the intricate workings of God's creation. Driven by the discoveries of Sir Isaac Newton and the empirical theories of Francis Bacon in England, there was a growing interest in exploring and understanding nature. The American colonies, with their seemingly infinite varieties of plant and animal life, offered a treasure trove for discoverers and scientists. One such man was William Wood, a British naturalist, who traveled the colonies cataloging the trees and wildlife of the frontier. He published his findings back in England, to the astonishment of scientific authorities who marveled at the variety and sheer quantity of species. Now directly in touch with nature, men like Wood began to look at it in new ways, through new eyes.

This drive for scientific understanding led to another crucial cultural advance—the interaction of civilization and the frontier. Prior to the settlement of America, few Europeans had actually come into contact with the vast and rich resources of the frontier. But the succeeding waves of immigrants to the New World exposed thousands, and eventually millions, to the apparently unlimited abundance of these new lands. Bringing advanced European technologies to this virgin territory formed an environment where new applications for the existing technology were developed, allowing the colonies to actually leapfrog European industry.

THE MOTHER OF INVENTION

Frontier ingenuity developed a system by which raw materials could be transformed into usable products almost instantaneously. In Europe, wood was an increasingly rare commodity, but in the New World, there was an almost endless supply immediately at hand. There were also countless streams and rivers available to effortlessly transport trees after they had been cut down. These waterways then provided the power, via waterwheel sawmills, to turn a tree into lumber for any number of purposes.

An entire industry, which could have never existed in Europe, was created from scratch to literally build a new country with affordable housing and commercial buildings. This new condition guaranteed all manner of economic opportunities for the colonists.

Creating a culture of innovation also served the more practical purpose of dramatically improving agricultural methods. Not only were the colonies able to feed themselves, but they could also send food and other cultivated products, like cotton and tobacco, to the far reaches of the world. This, in turn, birthed a whole new class of entrepreneurs, traders, and merchants who were able to invest in their colonial businesses and spend money on the products coming from the emerging class of American craftsmen.

The abundance of processed materials available to the burgeoning population also spawned a class of craftsmen who created new and improved products for use both in the colonies and back in England. No longer subject to the medieval artisan guilds of Europe, which had kept many creative workers locked out of the middle class, American craftsmen were now free to create and improve their trades without running afoul of the aristocratic order. The guild restrictions that prevented them from entering a trade no longer existed, and the craftsmen could practice their callings and skills regardless of their social rank. They could also now create their own art forms since they were not bound by the terms and tastes of royal patrons. Instead, they were able to gear their works to the demands of the marketplace.

The abundance of inexpensive, raw, and processed materials allowed colonial craftsmen to experiment with new methods and sell products cheaply in the markets created by the expanding colonies. Thus, many of the luxuries that were available only to ministers of state in England were immediately at hand and affordable to merchant families in America. The silver industry of Boston, for instance, produced the finest silver work in the British Empire—items that were once available only by royal prerogative could be owned by average, middle class Americans.

Furniture makers benefited from the cheap, processed lumber available only in the colonies. The watermills eliminated the need for large numbers of laborers to cut the lumber—which was necessary because of the shortage of labor that existed in virtually every colony. This also meant that since production costs were lower than in England, they could produce furniture more cheaply and in greater quantity. Because a craftsman could spend his time on the product itself, rather than preparing the materials, he had time to add ornaments, as well as personal flashes and flourishes. But these distinctive ornamentations did not distract from the pragmatic value of their art; it was beautiful, but it was also practical.

Craftsmen could also work for themselves. Glassblowers arrived in America from Venice and Poland to escape the artisan monopolies in their homelands, and, as a result, new methods of blowing, cutting, and arranging glass were developed that remained unique to the colonies. Pottery and ceramics, often reserved for the aristocracy in England, could be found in many colonial homes and put to all kinds of practical uses.

THE WRITE STUFF

But this colonial individuality and creativity was not limited to manufacturing; it was also expressed in the writings, music, and poetry of the new culture. Even the smallest cities and towns featured theater and music performances. Printing presses brought over from England began to churn out newspapers and books at a breathtaking pace, which was matched by the demand of the populace for information, education, and news. Surprisingly, the literacy rates in colonial America matched and surpassed those of modern times, and newspapers and publishers sprang up in every colony to service the booming port cities along the Atlantic coast.

One of the most famous newspaper publishers was Benjamin Franklin of Philadelphia. Acquiring the *Philadelphia Gazette* in 1729, he gained notoriety throughout the colonies with his annual compendium of folk wisdom, gardening recommendations, and weather charts, *Poor Richard's Almanac*. He was able to pontificate on politics, society, religion, science, and anything else that might strike his fancy. Franklin exemplified the new type of man that American colonial life had begun to produce—self-made, prolific, and the master of many interests. He engaged in a wide range of scientific experiments throughout his lifetime, ranging from the practical, such as developing household inventions, to the natural, including agricultural and geological discoveries. He was the consummate American Renaissance man.

Franklin rode the waves of success on the basis of a new cultural phenomenon—the celebrity. Widely renowned for his achievements in business, science, and public affairs, he basked in the limelight and indulged in the fruits of his popularity. Because of his fame, the intellectual elite on both sides of the Atlantic regularly courted him, and he made several trips to England to represent a variety of colonial interests. There he drank deeply from the cup of hedonism that London society offered and enjoyed being feted by the European upper crust.

It is important to note how crucial a role this celebrity culture played in the years leading up to the War of Independence. Had Franklin been born in England and experienced his printing success there, he would have scarcely garnered the slightest attention. There the social classes were properly defined and defended and Franklin would have gone unnoticed. While he would have been lost in the crowd anywhere in Europe, in America, he became a cultural icon. As conflict with England escalated, men like Franklin, Paul Revere, and Samuel Adams, who had risen to celebrity status, would make themselves heard, leading the new nation to a new future.

SALUTARY NEGLECT

One contributing factor to this birth of a uniquely American culture was the English administrative policy of "salutary neglect," which the colonies enjoyed until the years immediately preceding the War of Independence. With only a few rare exceptions, the colonies were left to develop on their own. This laissez-faire attitude extended not just to political affairs, but also to culture, law, religion, and economics.

From the beginning, the Crown had nothing to lose from the colonial ventures. Although the Stewart kings made massive land grants in the New World during the 17th century to their friends and political allies, those parties bore the full weight and risk of their investment. At no point did the Crown subsidize their colonies, unlike the Spanish and French. This markedly different English stance towards their colonies was reflective of their expansionist, decentralized, and Protestant tendencies. France, England's mortal enemy during this period, maintained a provincial, centrally controlled, and statist colonial policy. As tensions escalated between the French and the English during the "Old Wars" (1689-1763), these differences in colonial policy would play a crucial role as the conflict between England and France was played out at points all over the globe.

But salutary neglect was not nearly so much a deliberate strategy as it was a matter of default. During the one hundred-fifty years prior to the War of Independence, England was embroiled in the most difficult internal political battles in the country's existence. These political conflicts reflected the growing religious hostilities that were already tearing Western Europe apart. While the English monarchy was at its height during the Elizabethan and early Stuart eras, it eventually sundered the nation with civil war, fell out of power, was restored, suffered through a succession crisis, endured yet another civil war and several insurrections, and, in the end, was severely limited.

The difficulties began during the reign of James I, the successor of Elizabeth I. Since Elizabeth died in 1601 without an heir, the throne passed to her cousin, James Stuart, who was then Scotland's King James VI. While James had been raised under the tutelage of the leading Scottish Presbyterian divines of the day, he quickly adopted and acted on the Roman Catholic doctrine of the divine right of kings. An absolutist monarch, he passed on that heritage to his son, Charles I, who tried to enforce his will as law and ran headlong into a confrontation with Parliament over his rightful powers. In 1628, after attempting to raise taxes without consent of Parliament and jailing several of its members, Charles was forced to concede to the Petition of Right, which established the right of "no taxation without representation."

After his political thumping in 1628, Charles refused to call Parliament again until 1640, when he needed to raise money to defend the realm from a Scottish invasion. The Scots were responding to efforts by Archbishop Laud, primate of the Church of England, to overthrow Presbyterianism in their homeland in favor of Anglicanism. Parliament, once assembled, demanded redress of grievances and concession of powers by the Crown to Parliament in return for the authorization of funds.

At that time, Parliament was dominated by the Puritan party, who rejected the divine right theory and held that all authority was derived from God and could only be administered according to the limits proscribed by God's law. Charles would have none of that. He attempted to arrest several Puritan leaders of Parliament in violation of the law, and when Parliament refused to turn over the members, Charles dissolved the Parliament, which provoked the English Civil War in 1642.

After a long and bitter struggle, the Parliamentary forces prevailed over Charles and forced him to agree to relinquish some of his claims to power. Meanwhile, Charles attempted to raise Roman Catholic armies from France and Ireland to invade England and reclaim his throne. Once word leaked of the plan, Parliament formed a tribunal and tried the king for treason. Found guilty, he was beheaded on January 30, 1649, and Parliament abolished the monarchy and proclaimed England a Commonwealth. The rule of Parliament was little better than under Charles, which prompted Oliver Cromwell, the leading general of the Parliamentary armies during the Civil War, to take control of the country in 1653 and establish a Protectorate. Shortly after Cromwell died in 1658, the Stuart heir, Charles II, was able to rally support for a restoration of the monarchy. He returned to England and was crowned king in 1660.

When Charles II died without an heir, the throne passed to his brother, the Duke of York, who was crowned James II. James, who had evident Roman Catholic tendencies, was eventually ousted by Parliament in 1688 in the "Glorious Revolution." His daughter, Mary, and her husband William, the Prince of Orange in the Dutch Republic, were invited to come to England to reign as William III and Mary II.

When William and Mary also died without an heir, the throne fell to her sister, Anne, who outlived all 17 of her children. Rejecting the claims of all other Stuart heirs—including the son of James II—Parliament turned to a royal German alternative, George, the Elector of Hanover.

This cycle of political turmoil and repeated constitutional crises in England during the colonial era, combined with the international struggles with France and Spain, contributed to the administrative neglect of the American colonies. This allowed a great deal of self-government and fostered a healthy spirit of independence, freedom, liberty, and prosperity.

The original charters that authorized the colonies contained provisions that contributed to this remarkably independent spirit. While most colonies had governors appointed by the crown, the popularly elected representative assemblies controlled the purse strings of the treasuries. In time, the assemblies grew in power and prestige, bolstered by the talented colonial leaders that surfaced during that time.

Salutary neglect also insured that taxation and regulation policies were lax and, for long periods, non-existent. There were no real taxes assessed in the colonies until the reign of George III, who thought that the colonies should bear the financial burden of their defense during the Seven Years' War. This move by the king prompted the colonial assemblies to vehemently protest the change in policy. Protectionist regulations, such as the prohibition of selling wool hats in the colonies, were so ludicrous and impossible to police that they were flagrantly violated.

But the extent of salutary neglect was not limited to the political sphere; the social and cultural implications were just as important in the development of colonial society. In the religious realm, the Toleration Act guaranteed the rights of religious dissenters to worship according to their consciences. As a result, dissenters flocked to America from England, Ireland, and Scotland in the most massive population shifts in history up to that time and were left to engage in worship freely. They traveled to the New World as families and established thriving communities governed by the dictates of their respective religious beliefs.

When dissenters rose up in those communities, they were free to push outward into the frontier to establish their own settlements. Internal dissension in the colonies was significantly curbed by the fact that those who were discontented could vote with their feet. They were aided by the availability of cheap land in the colonies, so much so that farmers in America owned more land than the gentry back in England. The fact that the population was continually spreading outside the established boundaries meant the British government had an even more difficult time enforcing the king's edicts as the colonies grew in size and in number.

Another benefit of the unintentional neglect of the colonies was that they could transplant the English political and legal traditions while simultaneously transforming those systems to accommodate their needs and visions. They took full advantage of the "rights of Englishmen" that flourished back home in the 17th century. The colonials embraced the Right of Petition of 1628, the Bill of Rights of 1689, the Toleration Act, the Magna Carta, and the cherished Arbroath Declaration—the decree of Robert the Bruce in 1320 which enumerated the rights of ordinary men for the first time—as their rightful inheritance.

They also embraced the English common law tradition, which honors precedent and consent, and rejected the statist civil law tradition of continental Europe. But they also adapted the common law for use in the frontier, and they used the transfer of the common law from England to America as an opportunity to remove the feudal aspects left over from medieval times and the divine right accretions that had gathered during the Stuart era.

The most important aspect of transplanting the common law in America was the establishment of the rule of law. This fundamental concept in English law, which was enshrined in Henry de Bracton's famous 13th century dictum, "Not under man, but under God and law," was understood by the Americans to mean that any government official, including the king, had to act on the basis of the law and could not change the structure of the government or the laws without the consent of those governed. Furthermore, there were fixed standards of law established in God's decrees—found in the Bible—and in His created order—found in nature—that were to be obeyed by everyone, at all times. When George III and his ministers began to promulgate arbitrary regulations and taxes that contravened this well-established idea, the colonial leaders would directly appeal to the rule of law in defense of their protest and resistance.

The policy of salutary neglect would have far-reaching consequences for the British Empire. Severed from their motherland by a vast ocean, the colonies developed a culture that would eventually clash with the repeated shifts of English policy towards absolutism. They developed their own governmental structures and were left to defend themselves against the Indians, French, and Spanish. This created a self-reliance that proved to be essential, as the colonies needed to raise funds and militias to defend themselves against the English troops that would eventually arrive on their shores. They also developed a social, legal, and religious philosophy that grew out of the developments back home, but they created their own terms and interpretations that grew farther apart from the views in England. Unknown to the aristocrats and politicians in London, America was forging a unique culture.

A NEW KIND OF COLONY

The frontier experience and all the hardships and obstacles that the settlers had to face created a hearty, self-reliant character in those who survived the ocean voyage and the early years of suffering and starvation. But they were able to bring with them their traditions and hopes for a better life. Those who settled in New England and the South after fleeing religious persecution back home dreamed of creating a "city on a hill," a "New Jerusalem," and "Christian Commonwealth." And now that they were free to pursue those lofty ideals, they put them into action.

As the people of the British Empire extended their reach across the seas and around the globe, they brought England with them. But in the case of the American colonists, they brought their own England with them. They enjoyed the indifference that was extended to them as they birthed a new vision of what life apart from the monolithic, homogeneous, European culture could be. The result was a new kind of colony that was drastically different than any before or since.

There they developed competing visions of what an English colony should look like. The old model saw the colonies as little more than outposts where British merchants, protected from competition by monopolies granted by the crown, could plunder to collect sufficient raw materials to ship home. The only English inhabitants were small groups of traders who oversaw the system of spoils. No distinctly Western culture was ever established in those areas.

But the new model that developed in America was culturally aggressive and progressive. Creating something much more substantive than mere distant trading outposts, the colonists that arrived had their own cultural agendas. Bringing their families with them, they created wealth-producing communities that took advantage of the vast resources available from the frontier. Using homegrown ingenuity, they improved upon existing technology and created profitable industries. Rather than shipping the raw materials back to England, they processed them into final form right there. They constructed churches and formed schools, wrote poetry and literature, composed unique music, and built sprawling cities—all outside the view of the Crown. The colonists prayed, and they worked. They built a whole new culture—a literal New England, which was composed of a panoply of religious beliefs, ethnic backgrounds, customs, and opportunities.

This culture was created by the new kind of man that developed in the New World—industrious, hardy, independent, visionary, intellectual, pious—but not intolerant—innovative, and entrepreneurial. Ideas were important, but they were relevant only as the colonists did the real work of living their lives on the basis of this new worldview and in accordance with this new model of society. The colonies were no longer trading outposts; instead, they were living, breathing communities. Cities, such as Boston, New York and Philadelphia, became boomtowns as new commercial markets rose up within and between the colonies.

All this eventually led to the unprecedented founding of a new nation, conceived in both liberty and virtue, and confirming the establishment of the New World that was in almost every way different from the Old World.

DIVE DEEPER: COTTON MATHER

It is a cruel irony of history that Cotton Mather (1663-1728) is generally pictured unsympathetically as the archetype of a narrow and severe intolerance, who proved his mettle by prosecuting the Salem witch debacle of 1692. In fact, he never attended the trials—he lived in the distant town of Boston—and he actually denounced them once he saw the tenor they had taken. And as for his Puritanism, it was of the most enlightened sort. Mather was a man of vast learning, prodigious talent, and expansive interests. He owned the largest personal library in the New World—consisting of some 4,000 volumes and ranging across the whole spectrum of classical learning. He was also the most prolific writer of his day, producing some 450 books on religion, science, history, medicine, philosophy, biography, and poetry. His style ranged from *Magnalia Christi* Americana, dripping with allusions to classical and modern sources, to the practical and straightforward *Essays to Do Good*, which Benjamin Franklin claimed to be the most influential book ever written in this hemisphere.

He was the pastor of the most prominent church in New England—Boston's North Church. He was active in politics and civic affairs, serving as an advisor to governors, princes, and kings. He taught at Harvard and was instrumental in the establishment of Yale. He was the first native-born American to become a member of the scientific elite in the Royal Society, and was a pioneer in the universal distribution and administration of the small pox vaccine.

His father, Increase Mather, was the president of Harvard, a gifted writer, a noted pastor, and an influential force in the establishment and maintenance of the second Massachusetts Charter. In his day he was thought to be the most powerful man in New England—in fact, he was elected to represent the colonies before the throne of Charles II in London. But according to many historians, his obvious talents and influence actually pale in comparison to his son's.

Likewise, both of Cotton Mather's grandfathers were powerful and respected men. His paternal grandfather, Richard Mather, helped draw up the *Cambridge Platform*, which provided a constitutional base for the Congregational churches of New England. And with John Eliot and Thomas Weld, he prepared the *Bay Psalm Book*, which was the first text published in America. It achieved worldwide renown and remains a classic of ecclesiastical literature to this day. His maternal grandfather was John Cotton, who wrote the important Puritan catechism for children, *Milk for Babes* and drew up the *Charter Template* with John Winthrop as a practical guide for the governance of the new Massachusetts Colony. The city of Boston was so named in order to honor him—his former parish work in England was at St. Botolph's Boston.

According to historian George Harper, together these men laid the foundations for a lasting "spiritual dynasty" in America. Even so, according to his life-long admirer, Benjamin Franklin, "Cotton Mater [sic] clearly out-shone them all. Though he was spun from a bright constellation, his light was brighter still." He wrote more than 300 volumes. He represented the colonies to the crown. He helped to launch several vital educational institutions, including Yale—and all this while pastoring the most prominent church in New England. No wonder George Washington said, "He was undoubtedly the Spiritual Father of America's Founding Fathers."

DIVE DEEPER: LOST AMERICAS

Few today realize that the colonial period saw the establishment of several independent republics in and around the original American colonies. It was by no means a foregone conclusion that all of these would eventually give way to the continental hegemony of the United States—at least not to the pioneers who founded them.

Vermont was a region long disputed by the colonial governments of both New York and New Hampshire—but its residents always saw themselves as a breed apart. When the thirteen colonies issued their united Declaration of Independence, a small group of Vermont's leading citizens likewise issued a manifesto of secession. In the days that followed, they established a functioning republican form of government, elected representatives, and raised a militia. Under the judicious magistratal supervision of President Thomas Crittenden and the brash military prowess of Ethan Allen and his Green Mountain Boys, Vermont successfully confirmed its sovereign and free national status. Over the next fifteen years it operated as an entirely independent nation—even exchanging diplomatic delegations with the thirteen American states to the south and east. It was not until 1791 that the fiercely autonomous republic was enticed to join its fortunes with those of its neighbors under the newly ratified federal Constitution.

Likewise, the settlers along the Gulf Coast from Mobile Bay to the Mississippi River were rather disinclined to give up their sovereign status to join the American federal union. Under the presidency of Fulwar Skipwith—a distant relative of Thomas Jefferson—the residents of that isolated West Florida land established an independent republic and elected legislators to represent them at their capital, Baton Rouge. Though the Spanish and the English crowns disputed over the land, the settlers declared their sovereignty and set about the task of governance. It was not until 1810—when President James Madison dispatched troops from Louisiana to take possession of these Florida Parishes and forcibly annex them to the new American possessions nearby—that the "Bonnie Blue Flag" of the little nation was lowered and replaced by the "Stars and Stripes."

Of course, Franklin, the over-mountain settlement that grew out of the Watauga Association, engaged in its own struggle for independence. When the North Carolina legislature failed to make appropriate accommodations for the over-mountain communities, the residents called upon their leaders to interpose a magistratal jurisdiction that would truly represent them. As a result, a legislature was elected, and John Sevier assumed the office of the presidency. Though their first choice was to obtain admission to the American union as a new state, when their appeals seemed to fall on deaf ears, they asserted their sovereign national autonomy. Eventually, the residents were persuaded to merge their fledgling nation with the newly formed Tennessee territory, but their rugged individualism would forever set them apart.

What is striking about each of these early national experiments is that they were all driven by a fierce commitment to political freedom and liberty that grew naturally out of the Scots-Irish Presbyterianism of their respective residents. Though each was ultimately absorbed into the larger union—and though their distinctively Reformed character was gradually diluted by successive waves of new immigrants and new religious movements and traditions—their overall effect was lasting. Visit the Deep South of Mississippi and Alabama or the villages of taciturn Vermont and you will see evidence of that rugged independence. Though their unique American republics are no longer sovereign and independent, their impact upon us all is by no means lost.

CHAPTER 2: THE GREAT AWAKENING

*"The foundations of our society and our government rest so much on
the teachings of the Bible that it would be difficult to support them if
faith in these teachings would cease to be practically universal in our
country."*

CALVIN COOLIDGE

Despite the diverse backgrounds in all of the American
colonies, the Christian faith played a significant, if not
dominant, role in their founding and settling. Whether in the
Puritan holy commonwealths of New England, in the Cavalier
commercial establishments of the Middle Colonies, or in the
revivalist utopias of the South, each of the colonies was distinctly Christian in purpose, vision, and culture. Their charters, legal systems, social structures, commercial compacts, and political covenants were indisputably and unhesitatingly Christian.
America was founded on zeal for Christ and His Kingdom.

But as generations passed, the religious fervor that had led many to the New World began to fade, and church leaders across the colonies, particularly in New England, began to fret about the dampening of spiritual influence in the lives of the colonists. The malaise was predictable, if not understandable. The colonies were expanding and becoming more focused on matters of commerce and convenience. Personal peace and affluence became more important to many than the ideas and ideals that made such aspirations possible in the first place. As Cotton Mather asserted, the Christian faith had brought the colonies prosperity, but "the daughter destroyed the mother—there is a danger, lest the enchantments of this world make them forget their errand into the wilderness: to build a city on a hill, an illumination for all the world."

It seemed that there was little to disturb the colonists' pursuit of the "good life." Back in Britain, for instance, the succession crisis following the death of Queen Anne kept Parliamentary attentions diverted to the problems back home, leaving the colonies to themselves.

But even as Puritan pastors issued grave warnings and fierce jeremiads, a sudden renewal movement shook off the colonial spiritual malaise, swept across whole communities, and dramatically reshaped the cultural dynamics of the New World. The Great Awakening is the designation generally given to the series of revivals that occurred throughout the colonies in the period between 1720-1750, reaching its zenith toward the end of 1746 or the beginning of 1747. These revivals began on a small scale in the Connecticut River Valley and would sweep up and down the

Atlantic seaboard for the next few decades, reaching up to Maine and all the way down to Georgia.

The cumulative effects of this movement could be felt in the dramatic shift in communications, which resulted in closer relations of individuals, communities, and churches across the colonies. The theology that emerged from the Great Awakening redefined spiritual relationships, focusing more on the individual than on the community, creating ripple effects in the social and political structure of many colonies. It also created a common evangelical culture with a shared language that emphasized certain themes, such as liberty, virtue, and tyranny, which would take on more than just spiritual meaning in the years ahead. As historian Mark Shaw once said, "What was awakened in 1740 was the spirit of independence."

THE BUILDING WAVE

Though he was prefigured by many of the New England Puritan stalwarts who came before him, the first prominent figure of the Great Awakening was Jonathan Edwards. He was a Congregationalist pastor of the very prominent Puritan church in Northampton, Massachusetts. Edwards had assumed the pulpit upon the death of his grandfather, Solomon Stoddard, who had served as pastor for the church for many years and who had seen several periods of renewal in his own time. In late 1734, as Edwards was preaching a sermon on justification by faith, the members of his church began to be stirred by a conviction of their sin and a desire to live their lives more fully devoted and in obedience to Christ. Over the course of the next several weeks and months the town seemed to be transformed. Innumerable souls were converted. The church was crowded. Morals were discernibly altered. And then, the awakened spiritual affection in Northampton quickly spread to several neighboring towns in rural Massachusetts. Every aspect of life and culture seemed to come under the gracious influences of the Gospel.

Almost immediately, opinion amongst the clergy about the revivals was sharply divided. In response, Edwards authored a defense of the revivals, the *Faithful Narrative of the Surprising Work of God*, which described the events as nothing less than "the work of God." Copies of Edwards' revival account were soon circulating back in England, encouraging revival-minded pastors and raising concerns for the Anglican clergymen already troubled by their weak presence in America.

At about the same time in New Jersey, a Dutch Reformed pastor, Theodore Frelinghuysen, was seeing very similar responses in his church and the surrounding community as he preached on the need for a personal conversion experience, the necessity of holiness in the Christian life, and observing strict standards for admitting congregants to communion.

Similarly, William and Gilbert Tennant, father and son Presbyterian firebrands, thundered calls for the prosperous American colonial churches to humble themselves in true repentance. Their fire and brimstone message struck a chord, and they too saw hundreds of changed lives—and a dramatically changed culture as well.

The most comprehensive spiritual awakening since the time of the Reformation soon engulfed most of the colonies.

REVIVAL AFLAME

The watershed of the Great Awakening was the arrival of George Whitefield from England in 1738 to aid in the establishment of an orphanage in Georgia. He had recently graduated from Pembroke College at Oxford, where he developed a strong friendship with another student interested in living a deeper Christian life, John Wesley. He had become quite a celebrity back in England, having preached revival to enormous outdoor crowds in London and Bristol. Returning to England, he was ordained an Anglican pastor, and he returned to the colonies in 1739.

But it was on his tour of America in 1740 that the embers of revival would be fanned into full flame. Arriving in Savannah, he would preach to massive crowds in New York, Philadelphia, Boston, and Charleston, the largest cities at the time, and extensively tour New England from York, Maine to New Haven, Connecticut. He also found time to travel to the backwoods of Northampton to meet Jonathan Edwards and observe the work there.

The crowds gathered in fields, in town squares, and along roadsides. Numbering in the thousands at virtually every stop along the way, the throngs were attracted by Whitefield's unique preaching style. Rather than reading from his sermon notes, he spoke extemporaneously and with dramatic flair. Discarding the genteel and formal language of aristocratic society, he spoke openly and directly to the common man, which endeared him to the members of the lower classes. When the churches were closed to him or when the crowds grew too large for any building to hold, he would speak outdoors as he previously had in England. Many eager listeners traveled for days to hear him speak, and many thousands, spurred by Whitefield's message of the necessity of conversion, dedicated their lives to Christ.

Even diehard skeptics, like Benjamin Franklin, were impressed with the results of his preaching. "It was wonderful," Franklin said, "to see the change soon made in the manners of our inhabitants. From being thoughtless or indifferent about religion, it seems as if all the world were growing religious, so that one could not walk through the town in an evening without hearing psalms sung in different families of every street." While Franklin apparently never embraced the Christian faith, he maintained a friendship with Whitefield that lasted for years, became his American publisher, and promoted the cause of the awakening from that day forward.

Whitefield would eventually make seven trips to America over the next thirty-four years, dying during the last in September 1770. In that time, he would become the first celebrity recognized in every colony, in every region, and in every city in America. In the process, he would radically alter the spiritual landscape of the budding American nation.

A CHURCH DIVIDED

Now that revival was aflame throughout the colonies, few churches were left untouched. It was the topic of conversation at virtually every dinner table. The clergy began to be divided between those who wanted to embrace the revivals and integrate its popular message, called the New Lights, and those who rejected it entirely as mass hysteria. Some clergy, the Old Lights, saw it as a threat to the established social hierarchy and turned their back on the new converts. Although he was ordained as an Anglican, Whitefield frequently found those church doors closed to him. Once in Boston, a prominent Anglican minister expressed his disapproval directly, and said, "Mr. Whitefield, I am sorry to see you here," which prompted the revivalist to reply, "Yes, and so is the devil."

This exchange is indicative of how deep the faults within the American church were growing. While the Great Awakening was uniting rich and poor, young and old, and members of every religious group—Congregational, Baptist, Presbyterian, and Anglican—the revivals were also dividing people. While the movement would create an extensive evangelical culture that would allow pastors and churches of all backgrounds to work together, the different responses it provoked would create the divisions that would lead to the fracturing of several church organizations, spawning the denominational divisions that have marked American religious life ever since.

A NEW NATIONAL CALLING

Because of the growing national relevance of personal faith due to the effects of the Great Awakening, there was an increased awareness of how important religious liberty was to advancing the cause of Christ. The great Baptist leader of the time, Isaac Backus, emphasized that the gospel of grace could only take root in a culture that allowed for the freedom for it to be proclaimed. George Whitefield also often warned that political liberty could never be compromised without risking the integrity of spiritual liberty as well. He foresaw the danger that a conflict between the colonies and Britain might pose to the ongoing work of the gospel. Speaking to a crowd in Portsmouth, Massachusetts in 1764, he said: "I can't in conscience leave the town without acquaint-ing you with a secret. My heart bleeds for America. O poor New England! There is a deep-laid plot against both your civil and religious liberties, and they will be lost. Your golden days are at an end. You have nothing but trouble before you." He would not live to see how prophetic his words were.

The renewal movement not only awakened communities to spiritual and political realities, it also reinvigorated the rest of the culture through the recovery of the ideas of vocation and calling. The Reformers held that all Christians could participate in the building of the Kingdom of God, not just the ordained clergy, such that believers looked to conduct the whole of their lives in accordance with God's Word. This theme fit well with the Great Awakening's emphasis on the necessity of Christian obedience. Since the message of revival took root with all classes, workers and merchants alike labored with a new vigor in their occupations, filled with a sense of destiny and a calling to build a Christian society. As a result, craftsmen began to outshine their counterparts back in Europe, and entrepreneurs began building wealth to invest in the City of God.

Those touched by religious revival would wisely use those resources. One area toward which they were directed was the humanitarian concern that grew out of the interaction between people of differing ethnic, religious, and economic backgrounds. New attention was directed towards the plight of slaves, and an effort to end the practice began to take root. In fact, a ten-year old boy who heard one of Whitefield's last sermons, William Wilberforce, would grow up to single-handedly fight to end the practice in England. A missionary effort to evangelize the Indian tribes also grew out of the Great Awakening, as men like David Brainerd, a friend of Jonathan Edwards, ventured out into the wilderness to share the gospel with Indian tribes.

Educational institutions also sprang up as Christian leaders directed their attention to ensure that there were enough pastors to minister to the newly converted and to train cultural leaders to extend the benefits of the Christian message into all spheres of life. In 1726, as the first revivals were taking place, William Tennant founded the "Log College" to train pastors—pastors who became an active presence throughout the colonies as the Great Awakening took hold in the succeeding years. It would later become the College of New Jersey and then would be renamed Princeton. As the revival waves crashed along America's shores, religious organizations would found a number of other new colleges that are still important to our national life: Brown University, founded by Baptists in 1760; Queens College (later renamed Rutgers), a Dutch Reformed institution established in 1764; and Dartmouth College, founded by Congregationalist pastor Eleazar Wheelock in 1769.

SPIRITUAL REINFORCEMENTS ARRIVE

The Great Awakening had an enormous impact on the national life of the colonies, but its effects would be bolstered as a massive tide of Scots-Irish Presbyterian allies would appear on the American scene. The dimensions of the mass Scots-Irish exodus to America were staggering. Between 1725 and 1768, tens of thousands left Ireland for America. Nearly all were Protestants; most were Presbyterians. The migration began in 1714, and continued through 1717-1718, when Anglo-Irish landlords began to raise rents on the religious dissenters. Poor harvests and famines forced more to leave in 1728 and 1740-1741. In the later part of the 1740s, more than 12,000 a year would arrive on the shores of the New World.

Political troubles in Scotland were a contributing factor to the population shift. The defeat of the Stuart claimant to the English throne, Charles Stuart, known as "Bonnie Prince Charlie," and the massacre of his Scottish supporters at the Battle of Culloden in 1745 prompted George II to embark on a policy of clearing out the Scottish Highlands of his enemies. The purge of the Scottish clans from their lands and the suppression of traditional Scots culture—the old kilts, tartans, ballads, and even the Gaelic language—would drive many to the New World, putting distance between them and their religious and political enemies: the English. Between 1746 and 1766, nearly half the adult population of Scotland abandoned their homeland. For decades afterward, the stream of immigrants to America continued unabated in what came to be known as the Highland Clearances.

In terms of the Great Awakening, the timing could not have been more perfect. At the moment when the demand for trained pastors and church leaders was greatest and the revivals were at their peak, whole armies of catechized Presbyterians disembarked from ships arriving from Scotland and Northern Ireland. Despite their small populations, they would eventually outpace the English in relocating to America. Between 1763 and 1775, only 30,000 English immigrants would arrive in the colonies, compared to 95,000 Scots-Irish refugees. Not only did these new arrivals share the Calvinistic theological beliefs of Whitefield and Edwards, but they were also equally suspicious of the Anglican church establishment that had chased them from their homelands and were now denouncing the revivals in America.

No better marriage could have been made. The Presbyterians were welcomed enthusiastically by the revival leaders and immediately integrated into colonial society. They also served as shock troops to extend the religious movement as they settled along the frontier from the Georgia uplands into what is today Kentucky and Tennessee. By 1775, 200 new communities founded by the Scots-Irish immigrants blossomed in these areas, though they made their presence felt in established territories as well. Ben Franklin estimated in 1776 that there were 350,000 Presbyterians in Pennsylvania alone, representing one-third of the population of the entire colony. They also settled in the Shenandoah and Blue Ridge Valleys of Virginia, drastically altering the cultural landscape and setting the stage for a series of skirmishes with the established Anglican clergy there.

The arrival of the Scots-Irish in America flooded the revival movement with new workers and active supporters. As tensions between the colonies and Parliament escalated into armed conflict, it would be these communities that voiced their anti-imperial sentiments and banded together to organize the resistance. Since many of the Scots brought their military experience, along with their virulent hatred of the English, with them to America, they would play a key role in the establishment of the colonial militias. The War for Independence would vindicate many causes that had been fought and lost to the British in earlier conflicts back in the motherland.

THE OVERALL IMPACT

The Great Awakening would see many leaders rise up to take the challenge of evangelizing the world seriously. Because of the spiritual lethargy of the early 18th Century, the revivals were a breath of fresh air for the Christian church in the New World struggling to define its existence.

There were significant religious and theological consequences as a result of this tremendous movement of the Holy Spirit. Churches grew dramatically; involvement in churches by long-time members was greatly strengthened. The awakening encouraged personal obedience and holiness and revived the notion of Christian duty. It also served to create a unified evangelical culture. Despite continuing theological differences and distinctions, the communication and cooperation between the clergy and membership of a number of denominations increased, both locally and between colonies. A bond of fellowship was formed that would serve as a cultural glue in the years ahead.

In several cases, however, it could not keep religious groups from splitting apart. As the revivalist New Lights confronted and challenged the authority of the Old Lights, the two camps drifted further from each other. As the New Lights spoke of the religious impact on individuals, the Old Lights defended the church hierarchy as necessary to maintain social order. As the rift widened, the result was the birth of denominationalism, which ran counter to the unifying and cooperative trend of evangelicalism.

Vocalizing their opposition to the gospel of grace, the Old Lights began to reject the teachings of the Reformation and embrace Deism, which eventually drifted into Unitarianism in New England. Amongst the evangelicals, however, the popularized Calvinism of Whitefield and Edwards strengthened the burgeoning Baptist movement and reversed those churches' slide into Liberalism, Arminianism, and Unitarianism.

There were many cultural effects as well. The Great Awakening attracted young believers who would sustain the religious and cultural gains of the movement for several decades. The new colleges and educational institutions established by the revivalist religious groups would teach and train these leaders to integrate their new religious faith in every sphere of their lives.

Furthermore, those religious groups that held onto the revival teachings would grow much faster than the Anglican Church, which was hampered in their limited evangelistic efforts by the absence of any resident bishop—one who could have presided over and directed the church's affairs in the colonies—and the requirement of those seeking to enter the ministry to travel to England for their education and ordination. This would prove to be a significant barrier as other denominations trained their best and brightest in America and put them immediately in the field where they were needed.

Thus, much of the population would grow distant from the English church-state establishment and grow to resent it. This embedded dissent in America would manifest itself later, as the colonials grew increasingly hostile to any established religion. This did not mean that they were hostile to the Christian faith— quite the contrary—but it did contribute to a trend of secularization that would take hold later in the 18th Century.

New missionary zeal was aimed at the frontier communities, the Native American Indians, and the transplanted Africans— both slave and free. The awakened church was much more evangelistic and mission-minded than ever before, and thus, the hallmark of evangelicalism became a dominating distinctive of American life.

The Great Awakening also exposed the cultural decay in New England Puritan society, which had lost its way since the first generation of founders who came to America intent on building a Christian commonwealth. And while that was still a noble cause, the Calvinistic social theory those cultures were built from, which emphasized community as much as the individual, would later be replaced by Enlightenment teaching, which would transfer the struggle for a virtuous society from the religious to the political realm.

FORMATION OF A NATION

Possibly the greatest impact of the Great Awakening was the creation of an American nation—as a social reality if not yet a political reality. The colonies, with different governments, geography, climate, industry, and heritage, began to coalesce into a cultural whole. A whole new mode of popular communication that broke with the formal modes of discourse and transcended class distinctions now traveled along networks that extended from the cities to the very edges of the frontier. The revivals affected virtually every region of the country and had ripples that extended into a number of areas of life. Unfortunately, several regions, such as Canada, at this time still under the domination of the French, and the Gulf Coast colonies in the South, missed the revivals and the associated cultural benefits.

This new nation would be established on the basis of a common religious and political vision and would develop a comprehensive vocabulary of freedom, which was characterized by a dominant theme of virtue in religion and government. A letter published by the *Virginia Gazette* in June 1769 embodies this hope, for it says: "The prevailing principle of our government is virtue [...]. We must be more attentive to it than we hitherto have been: By that only can liberty be preserved [...]. By virtue, I here mean a love for our country, which makes us pursue, with alacrity, such measures as tend to its preservation, and cheerfully resist the temptations of ease and luxury with which liberty is incompatible."

During this time, the emerging American nation would develop a kind of national creed. It would be expressed in a language of liberty it appropriated from the Great Awakening—freedom from tyranny, personal responsibility, and a life of action. While the revivalists never could have anticipated the application of their religious principles to the cultural and the political, these themes would thunder as commands from the revolutionary pulpits in the decades to come. The religious revivals provoked a colossal shift in identity in the colonies as the attachments to the Old World eroded and as colonists challenged their existing allegiances while the conflicts in Europe drifted to the New World. The Great Awakening announced a new era in history. As historian Richard Bushman concluded in his book, *From Puritan to Yankee*, "A psychological earthquake had reshaped the human landscape."

DIVE DEEPER: GEORGE WHITEFIELD

He was America's first celebrity. Though just twenty-five years old when he began touring the sparsely settled colonies in 1738, George Whitefield (1714-1770) was an immediate sensation. And he remained so for the rest of his life. Over the next thirty years, amidst some seven visits from his native England, he would leave his mark on the lives of virtually every English-speaking soul living on this side of the Atlantic—from the cosmopolitan businessmen of Philadelphia and the seasoned traders of Boston to the yeomen farmers of Virginia and the frontier adventurers of Canada.

He took America by storm. "When he arrived in the colonies," says historian Mark Noll, "he was simply an event." Wherever he went, vast crowds gathered to hear him. Commerce would cease. Shops would close. Farmers would leave their plows mid-furrow. Affairs of the greatest import would be postponed. One of his sermons in the Boston Common actually drew more listeners than the city's entire population. Another, in Philadelphia, spilled over onto more than a dozen city blocks. Still another, in

Savannah, recorded the largest single crowd ever to gather anywhere in the colonies—despite the scant local population.

Some said he blazed across the public firmament like a "heav-
enly comet." Some said he was a "magnificent fascination of the
like heretofore unknown." Others said he "startled the world
awake like a bolt from the blue." There can be little doubt that
he lived up to his reputation as the "marvel of the age." As historian Harry Stout has written, "He was a preacher capable of com-
manding mass audiences—and offerings—across two continents,
without any institutional support, through the sheer power of
his personality. Whitefield wrote best-selling journals and drew
audiences totaling in the millions. White and black, male and
female, friends and enemies—all flocked in unprecedented numbers to hear the Grand Itinerant. Whenever he visited, people
could do anything, it seemed, but stay away."

By all accounts, he was the "father of modern evangelism."
He sparked a revival of portentous proportions—the Great Awakening; he pioneered one of the most enduring church reform
movements—Methodism; and he laid the foundations for perhaps the greatest experiment in liberty the world has yet known—
the American Republic.

All the greatest men of the day were in unabashed awe of his
oratorical prowess. Shakespearean actor David Garrick said, "I
would give a hundred guineas if I could say *oh* like Mr. Whitefield." Benjamin Franklin once quipped, "He can bring men to
tears merely by pronouncing the word *Mesopotamia*." And Sarah
Edwards—the astute and unaffected wife of the dean of American
theologians, Jonathan Edwards—remarked, "He is a born orator."

But he was equally beloved for his righteous character. George Washington said, "Upon his lips the Gospel appears even to the coarsest of men as sweet and as true as, in fact, it is." Patrick Henry mused, "Would that every bearer of God's glad tidings be as fit a vessel of grace as Mr. Whitefield." And the poet, John Greenleaf Whittier wrote of him:

"That life of pure intent,
That voice of warning, yet eloquent,
Of one on the errands of angels sent."

Yet despite his wide acclaim and popularity, Whitefield was often ridiculed, scorned, and persecuted for his faith. Hecklers blew trumpets and shouted obscenities at him as he preached. Enraged mobs often attacked his meetings, robbing, beating, and humiliating his followers. Men were maimed. Women were stripped and occasionally raped. Whitefield himself was subjected to unimaginable brutality—he was clubbed twice, stoned once, whipped at least half a dozen times, and beaten a half a dozen more. And he lived constantly under the pall of death threats. Once, he recorded in his journal, "I was honored with having a few stones, dirt, rotten eggs, and pieces of dead cats thrown at me. Nevertheless, the Lord was gracious, and a great number were awakened unto life."

Amazingly, it was not just the profane that condemned Whitefield's work. He was also opposed by the religious establishment. Accused of being a "fanatic," of being "intolerant," and of "fanning the flames" of "vile bigotry," he was often in "more danger of attack from the clergy than he was from the worldly."

As a result, biographer Arnold Dallimore says, "Whitefield's entire evangelistic life was an evidence of his physical courage." He fearlessly faced his opposition and continued his work. Though often stung by the vehemence of the opposition he faced, he refused to take it personally, attributing it rather to the "offense of the Gospel."

Thus, despite the fact that Whitefield obviously struck a sensitive chord and won a wide following among the people when he proclaimed the old Puritan doctrines of grace, he just as obviously stirred up fierce opposition among both the ungodly and the religious—who always have been and always will be united in their animosity toward the Gospel.

DIVE DEEPER:
JONATHAN EDWARDS

Unlike his friend George Whitefield, Jonathan Edwards (1703-1758) was not a particularly enthralling master of pulpit theatrics or preaching technique. Instead, he won his reputation as a thinker. He was highly regarded as a "precise dogmatician"; he was widely admired as a "careful systemizer"; and he was deeply appreciated as a "cogent preceptor."

As a philosopher, his greatness was unmatched. Thomas Chalmers said that he was "undoubtedly the greatest of all the theologians." Benjamin Franklin said that he "had a rational mind unmatched for generations untold." Daniel Webster said that his books were among the "greatest achievements of the human intellect." James Hollister said he was "the most gifted man of the eighteenth century, perhaps the most profound thinker in the world." Robert Hall said that "he was the greatest of the sons of men." Moses Tyler said he was "the most original and acute thinker yet produced in America." And Georges Lyon said he was "superior to Locke, Newton, Descartes, and a couple of Pascals combined."

But as a preacher, he apparently left a little something to be desired. In fact, he read his densely theological and tautly philosophical sermons from painstakingly researched, long-hand manuscripts—often in a flat, monotonous voice. Only rarely did he deign to make eye contact with his congregation. Though not unpleasant in demeanor, he hardly cut a dashing or charismatic figure.

A member of his church described these deficiencies sympathetically: "His appearance in the pulpit was with a good grace, and his delivery easy, natural, but very solemn. He had not a strong voice but appeared with such gravity, and spake with such distinctness and precision--his words so full of ideas and set in such a plain and striking light--that few speakers have been so able to demand the attention of an audience as he. His words often discovered a great degree of inward fervor, without much noise or external emotion, and fell with great weight on the minds of his hearers. He made but little motion of his head or hands in the pulpit, but spake as to discover the motion of his own heart, which tended in the most natural and effectual manner to move and affect others."

But another said, "I can little explain how the assembly remains awake during his discourses—which are over-long, boorish, and often incomprehensible to the simple man. Though there is evidence of some great passion in thought, yet to the eye and ear, little or none."

Nevertheless, on July 8, 1741, Edwards traveled a few miles from his home into western Connecticut and read, to a small congregation assembled there, "the most famous sermon ever delivered in the history of America."

Entitled *Sinners in the Hands of An Angry God*, the sermon was an exposition of the text, "Their foot shall slide in due time" (Deuteronomy 32:35). Its subject was the imminence of judgment and the horrors of perdition. It was about what we today derisively call "hell-fire and damnation."

Later described by literary and historical critics as a "rhetorical masterpiece," the sermon was astonishingly gripping and terrifyingly vivid: "Yea, God is a great deal more angry with great numbers that are now on the earth; yea doubtless, with many that are now in this congregation, who it may be are at ease, than He is with many of those who are now in the flames of Hell. The wrath of God burns against them, their damnation does not slumber; the pit is prepared, the fire is made ready; the furnace is now hot ready to receive them; the flames do now rage and glow; the glittering sword is now whet and held over them. Unconverted men walk over the pit of Hell on a rotten covering, and there are innumerable places in this covering so weak that they will not bear their own weight, and these places are not seen."

The sermon caused an immediate sensation in the town of Enfield where it was preached. According to historian John Currid, even before the sermon was finished, "people were moaning, groaning and crying out" such things as "What shall I do to be saved?" In fact, there was such a "breathing of distress and weeping" that Edwards had to quiet and calm the people several times so he could conclude. The fervor of the Great Awakening that had thus far by-passed Enfield, now swept through the little town with a white-hot intensity. Suddenly, the people were "bowed down with an awful conviction of their sin and danger," and a "great outpouring of the Holy Spirit" came with "amazing and astonishing power," evidenced by the fact that "several souls were wrought upon" in that place of "former antipathy."

In short order, the sermon was printed and widely distributed throughout the Americas. It not only won for Edwards even greater renown than he already enjoyed, but it provoked a further awakening among its distant readers. Since then it has been reprinted hundreds of times—perhaps thousands. To this day it is not only a standard text for the study of great preaching; it has passed into the realm of classic literature—and as a result is the most anthologized sermon in the English language.

CHAPTER 3: INTERNATIONAL CONFLICT

"It is often so with institutions already undermined: they are at their most splendid external phase when they are ripe for downfall."

HILAIRE BELLOC

Throughout most of the colonial period, the British settlers in America enjoyed the benefits of "salutary neglect" due to England's internal and external conflicts. In many cases, the British government was glad to be rid of troublesome religious and political dissenters in the midst of their conflicts with the Dutch, French, and Spanish. Occasionally, the European conflicts would spill over into America, as they did in the Seven Years' War, over colonial territorial claims, but much of the contest between these early "superpowers" was over what nation and what religion would control European society and politics.

The international hostilities at the time were rooted in the disintegration of the old feudal and medieval order of Christendom. For hundreds of years, local rulers of small principalities, kingdoms, and duchies were subject to regional overlords, who were covenantally bound to overlords and kings. These political arrangements were gradually transformed into an inflexible and increasingly fragmented system involving the vast imperial ambitions of the Hapsburgs, the Bourbons, the Hohenzollerns, the Tudors, the Stuarts, and the Papacy.

Then came the Reformation, beginning with Martin Luther in 1517, which shattered the religious and political stasis altogether. The Holy Roman Empire, which was the locus of much of the European political power, soon disintegrated. Many political leaders, now free from their duties to the Emperor, took advantage of misfortunes of the Roman Catholic Church and consolidated their power into nation-states by making religion a political dynamic in their realms. The best example is England itself, where Henry VIII, who was refused a divorce from Catherine of Aragon by the Pope, severed all ties with Rome, proclaimed himself head of the Church of England, and issued a decree for his own divorce. Hardly a reformer in the religious sense, Henry VIII had just a few years earlier received the title "Defender of the Faith" from the Pope for writing a religious tract attacking Martin Luther and his followers. But his recalcitrance had nearly the same effect as that of Luther.

This realignment of religious and political powers led many other kings to extend their dominions by marriages and alliances to create their own empires free from religious oversight. Soon, these new nations were at war with each other as they scrambled to increase their power in Europe and claim new territories in the New World, which had been discovered in 1492 by

Christopher Columbus sailing under the Spanish flags of the kingdoms of Aragon and Castille.

The Dutch, who had won their independence from Spain in 1581 under William of Orange and had grown into a prosperous seafaring nation with excellent means of trade, had acquired a large territory in America, which they called New Netherlands. England wanted that same land, and they fought for it in the Anglo-Dutch War of 1652-54 after England passed the Navigation Act of 1651, which prevented the American colonist from trading with the Dutch. The Second Anglo-Dutch War was provoked when Charles II granted a charter to his brother, the Duke of York, under the condition that the Duke would drive off the Dutch "squatters." In 1664, he was successful, and he renamed the area New York. The two countries would square off again in a third war, which concluded with a peace treaty in 1674 and eliminated any Dutch claims in the New World.

England had more enemies to think about in Hapsburg Aragon and Castille and in France. The Hapsburgs had attempted to invade England with the Spanish Armada during the reign of Queen Elizabeth I, but they failed and saw their power diminished considerably. They continued to make claims in the New World along the southern coast of North America. To counter this Spanish threat, General James Oglethorpe was granted a charter by George I to establish a colony in the south, called Georgia, to insulate the rest of the English colonies from the Hapsburg lands in and around the Gulf of Mexico and the threat of Spanish raids.

But England's long-time nemesis was France. The monarchs of each country had made opposing claims in the other's country going back to the Norman invasion of England by William the Conqueror in 1066. The first Hundred Years' War, during the 14th and 15th centuries, was fought between England and France over these competing claims. There were also internal power struggles during this period, primarily in England in the War of the Roses, between the Houses of York and Lancaster. But the cessation of hostilities at the end of the Hundred Years' War did not curb the conflict between England and France.

Moreover, France had internal political troubles of its own. The Reformation had divided the country in two: the French Protestants, the Huguenots, were from wealthy and powerful families of the South and struggled for power with the Roman Catholics, who represented the majority of the Parisians and the North. This resulted in the French Wars of Religion, which were resolved by the Edict of Nantes that granted toleration to the Huguenots. When Louis XIV revoked the edict, the Huguenots were driven from France to Europe, England, and the New World. Many would settle in New York, New Jersey, and western Pennsylvania.

Religious wars flared up in England as well. The English Civil War, between the Parliament—controlled by the Puritan party—and Charles I, raged for almost a decade, until the Parliamentary forces emerged victorious, tried Charles for treason, and beheaded him in January 1649. The king's son, Charles II, would return as king in 1660 to a deeply divided England. At the time of his death, his brother, James II, a Roman Catholic, was crowned king. But religious and political conflicts with Parliament led to James being overthrown in the Glorious Revolution of 1688 and William and Mary being brought from the Netherlands to rule the country jointly.

THE SUN KING

It was this development that escalated tensions between England and France. Louis XIV, the French monarch, had supported Charles II in his attempt to reclaim the English throne. Now that James II, married to a French princess, had been sent packing, Louis felt compelled to react. He saw James's removal as a humiliation to all of France and a setback for their Roman Catholic Faith, and he refused to recognize William and Mary as lawful rulers of England, conspiring to return James II to the throne.

There was more to Louis's defense of James than personal attachments. It represented a conflict of visions that would manifest itself as a second Hundred Years' War between England and France; a war played out all over the globe until the defeat of Napoleon at the Battle of Waterloo in 1815. Louis was driven by the humanist philosophy of the Divine Right of Kings, which, though sounding religious, is in fact just the opposite. This is the belief that the king is the sole representative of God on the earth, and is subject to no one, whether in church or state. This theory was birthed out of the Italian Renaissance, which rejected biblical Christianity for a new religion of humanity and the belief in infinite progress, and was seized on by European kings hungry for power after the dissolution of the Holy Roman Empire.

One of the first defenders of this dogma was James I of England, who rejected his Protestant upbringing and forcefully defended his right to act as god in his realm. He taught his son, Charles, to reign in the same manner. James' boyhood tutor, the Scottish Reformer George Buchanan, had authored a treatise early in James's reign, *On the Powers of the Crown of Scotland*, which made the case for a limited monarchy. James responded by authoring his *Defense*

of True and Lawful Monarchy, in defense of his divine right. Decades later, another Scottish pastor, Samuel Rutherford, would
pen a work, *Lex, Rex* or "The Law and the Prince," which would
argue against the prevailing theory of the divine right of kings and
state that all monarchs are bound by oath to objective constitutional standards. Charles II found the book an affront to his claim
to the throne and summoned Rutherford to appear before a royal
tribunal to defend his writings in 1661. Rutherford escaped execution only by dying on the way to the trial. The Glorious Revolution would eventually resolve the debate of divine right monarchy
in England, but it would continue to gain adherents in Europe.

LIVING LIKE A GOD

In France, Louis wanted to make a bold statement about his
powers as a divine right monarch. Styling himself as "the Sun
King" and creating a cult of personality, he spent enormous
amounts of public money on grand displays of music, art, and
culture that mirrored his grandiose ideas of himself. But his
most significant piece of propaganda was the construction of
his mammoth palace at Versailles. Unlike any other palace of
the time, it was a sprawling (and expensive) complex, with hundreds of rooms to house thousands of courtiers and servants
and a man-made lake with extravagant fountains and Venetian
gondolas to transport members of the royal court down the
canals to the remote areas of the estate. There he would host
grand balls and preside over daily celebrations dedicated to his
power and glory. There was also a practical purpose for Versailles—he needed to keep all of his political competitors close
to him, as rival factions of the Houses of Orleans, Bourbon,

and Burgundy vied for power in France. With his enemies close at hand, and the public awed at the spectacle and magnificence of his palace and of his reign, he justified his claim to divine authority by acting like a god. In the next century in the French Revolution, the lower classes would voice their resentment over having to pay for the King's extravagance and show him that he was not a god by cutting off his head.

Back in England, the Glorious Revolution of 1688 had secured a constitutional government and had passed the Toleration Act and the Bill of Rights of 1689 to protect the religious and civil liberties of the English people—quite the contrast from the autocratic Roman Catholic regime across the English Channel in France. Arriving in England, William and Mary began to coordinate their military response to Louis by allying with their supporters in Holland and several other small German states, who were also concerned about the threat of French aggression in Europe. This alliance, the League of Augsburg, would play a central role in the upcoming struggle between England and France that would be played out in both the Old and the New World.

CONFLICTS OF FUR AND FURY

In America, there had been conflict between the English and the French from the outset. The English had been in Jamestown barely a year when the French arrived to settle what became Quebec, New France. By the time the French and English were bickering in Europe over which king should be sitting on what throne, the French and English colonists had spent nearly a century arguing over religion, land, and especially the valuable fur trade. In 1689, both sets of colonists were competing for fur trade with the Indians. The French formed an alliance with the Huron tribes, which spread from the Great Lakes east to Acadia (the early name for Nova Scotia). The English found a natural alliance with the Iroquois confederation of tribes because the Iroquois had a long history of conflict with the Hurons. The Five Nations of the Iroquois Confederation—later to be called the Six Nations when the Tuscarora joined the confederation—dominated the territory that is now central New York.

HAIRY BUSINESS

Most of the French who came to the New World were single young men who came to trade in furs. They took Indian wives and even adopted much of Indian culture. These Frenchmen were called *voyageurs* or *coureurs de bois*. The *voyageurs* (whose name, as you might suspect, means "voyagers") traveled as far away from New France as the Pacific coast or the Gulf of Mexico. The *coureurs de bois* (which means "forest runners") might not venture any further away from Quebec than a few hundred miles. Both groups made their living in the fur trade and dealt regularly with the Indians.

To protect this valuable trade, the French built a chain of forts, which stretched from the mouth of the St. Lawrence River in New France to the mouth of the Mississippi River at the Gulf of Mexico in French Louisiana.

The English felt sure that if any kind of conflict arose, they would have the advantage because they vastly outnumbered the French. However, they overlooked an important strength of the French: a strong, centrally organized government. The test would come soon enough as France and England began to pit their strengths against one another in a series of colonial battles.

KING WILLIAM'S WAR

War broke out in the colonies in 1680 when Iroquois Indians invaded the west and massacred a tribe of Indians known as the Illinois. The Iroquois had hoped to win over the western Indians from their French allies and take their fur trade away from the French. The French responded six years later by attacking a Hudson Bay Company outpost used to slip furs past the French and into English hands. In 1689, some fifteen hundred Iroquois warriors attacked the village of La Chine, only six miles from Montreal, in the most savage massacre in Canadian history. At almost that very moment, the War of the League of Augsburg broke out in Europe between France and England. The English colonists named their own extension of the war, King William's War, in honor of their new monarch.

King Louis immediately sent the aging, but competent, Count Frontenac (1620-98) back to Canada to take charge. He returned to a colony close to collapse. Frontenac immediately launched a three-pronged attack against the English to impress the Iroquois with the power of New France. In February 1690, French troops burned the village of Schenectady to the ground, slaughtering sixty settlers and capturing a hundred more in the process.

Frontenac had been aided by the turmoil within the English colonies themselves. Massachusetts had recently jailed Governor Andros and was living under a disunited provisional government, while New York was occupied with Leisler's Rebellion. The French and Indian raids shocked the English colonies and spurred them on to plan an inter-colonial invasion of the Canadian provinces.

Seven vessels under the command of Sir William Phips (1651-95), a future governor of Massachusetts, sailed from Boston to Port Royal, Acadia, which quickly surrendered not only the fort, but also control of the entire peninsula of Acadia.

The inter-colonial invasion of Canada, however, failed miserably. Fearing Frontenac's power, most of the English Iroquois allies stayed home, while the colonial leaders quarreled among themselves. At Quebec, several skirmishes exhausted the English supply of ammunition, so Phips gave up and returned home, unaware that the French were short of food and would likely have surrendered if he had remained much longer. The war dragged on for seven more years. Frontenac recaptured Port Royal and drove the English traders from their posts on Hudson Bay. Sensing the nearly total lack of leadership and cooperation in the English colonies, the Iroquois nearly deserted to the French. Fortunately for the English, the Peace of Ryswick of 1697 ended the war in Europe, and thus the war in America.

The bloody colonial war had solved nothing, but it had left a bitter legacy of mutual hatred between the French and the English colonists that would leave no room for anything but total victory for one or the other.

FRANCE AND SPAIN, HAND IN HAND

In 1701, events in Europe once again struck the American colonies. The powerful French king, Louis XIV, placed his grandson, Philip of Anjou, upon the now united Spanish thrones of Aragon and Castille. England was gravely concerned because the union of these staunch Roman Catholic countries gave Louis control over a vast proportion of Europe's power and wealth and trapped the English colonies in America between two hostile empires. England responded by declaring war on France in May 1702. This war became known in Europe as the War of Spanish Succession. It spread at once to the American colonies where it came to be called Queen Anne's War after the new English monarch.

The French began by stirring up the fierce Abnaki Indians, who reportedly engaged in cannibalism, against settlements on the New England frontier. In 1703, they raided Wells, Maine, butchering thirty-nine settlers, mostly women and children. The following year, raiding parties hit Deerfield, Massachusetts, murdering thirty-eight settlers and leading off another hundred into captivity in the hopes of getting ransom money. One survivor of the Deerfield Massacre, John Williams, was held prisoner for two years. After being freed, he wrote *The Redeemed Captive Returning to Zion*, which, like Mary Rowlandson's narrative of her captivity, became a best seller.

French privateers harassed colonial shipping all along the Atlantic coast. Soldiers from the Carolinas destroyed Spanish Saint Augustine but failed to capture its formidable stone fort. They later destroyed over a dozen Spanish missions along the Gulf Coast. Spanish and French raided Charleston and Americans raided Pensacola, but the war in the South mostly degenerated into duels between privateers.

In 1713, the Treaty of Utrecht ended the fighting in the colonies as well as in Europe.

JENKINS'S EAR

By the 1730s, British smuggling and piracy in the West Indies had led to a small, undeclared naval war, which the Hapsburg Spanish were winning. One victim of the hostilities was Robert Jenkins, a British smuggler who had lost an ear when soldiers from a Spanish vessel had boarded his ship off the coast of Florida. Jenkins had preserved his ear, and when he returned to England, he took every opportunity to show off this grisly reminder of his unfortunate encounter with the Spanish. Parliament saw the loss of Jenkins's ear as an insult to British honor and a sufficient cause to go to war.

The War of Jenkins' Ear (1739-1743) was fought primarily between Spanish Florida and General Oglethorpe's Georgia colony. Within a few years, however, the conflict disappeared into a much broader war, the War of the Austrian Succession (1740-1748), as it was called in Europe, and King George's War (1744-1748), as it was called in America in honor of King George II.

It began in Europe after Queen Anne's War was over, when royal families in Europe again began quarreling over the right of succession. The quarrel escalated into a war involving most of Europe. The colonists in America—both English and French— were soon caught up in the conflict as well.

CHAAAARGE!

Although King George's War was little more than occasional raids between frontiersmen and Indians, there was one major campaign by the English colonists against France's mighty Fort Louisbourg on Cape Breton Island. This fort was on a strategic point, just north of Acadia overlooking the Gulf of the St.

Lawrence River. The English knew that Louisbourg would be a perfect site to launch an invasion from French-controlled Canada. Governor William Shirley of Massachusetts helped plan the expedition, which was led by Colonel William Pepperell of Maine. Pepperell gathered a force of ninety vessels carrying four thousand soldiers who had been recruited from the New England colonies. For a month and a half, Pepperell's troops laid down a siege at Louisbourg, firing more than three thousand cannonballs into the fort. On June 17, 1745, the strongest fort in North America surrendered to the New England militiamen.

The French sought revenge by sending out a fleet, but a gale forced it to return home before attacking the British. A second fleet was likewise scattered, this time by a superior British force. The French and their Indian allies were now carrying out a series of destructive raids in Maine. They also besieged New York, where they burned down the English Fort Saratoga and launched an unsuccessful attack on the colonial capital of Albany.

AS YOU WERE

By 1748, France and England were thoroughly weary of war. They signed the Treaty of Aix-la-Chapelle, which restored the land to the original owners. However, in order for France to regain her prized Fort Louisbourg, she had to give up control of the port of Madras, India.

After the huge expense and suffering that this war had caused the English colonists, they were extremely bitter that a treaty signed on the other side of the ocean made them give Louisbourg back to France. Even the £235,000 that Parliament sent to the colonies to repay their expenses did not ease their disappointment.

By giving up Louisbourg, England lost her chance to capture all of Canada and lost the goodwill of many of her colonists.

A CLASH OF CULTURES

This series of repeated military exchanges between England and France marks the clash of the two cultures. In England, the Glorious Revolution had established a constitutional monarchy. In France, absolutism reigned. But there was more than politics involved. Both countries had distinct and contrary policies regarding the colonies. The British Empire was decentralized and expansive, while a centralized, provincial spirit stymied the growth of civilization and hampered the French colonial efforts. Whereas the French had economic motives in mind for their settlements, inhabited primarily by single men, many of the English colonies were religious havens for families. Because English colonial culture was built on the stable foundation of permanent communities, British society could take root in the New World.

An emerging ideology of "Britannia" swept England and the colonies during this period and would provoke an upsurge in patriotic fervor in America during the Seven Years' War. But the colonists' nationalist hopes would be dashed as they discovered that their identity as Englishmen, entitled to all the respective rights thereof, was rejected by the aristocratic elite back home. The nationalist intentions of the British Empire would be brought to bear on America as English soldiers would be brought in under the guise of protecting the colonies, but actually with the intention of suppressing them.

The Old French Wars were the product of a revival of animosities that began with the unraveling of the old European order and would continue all the way through the 18th century. The Seven Years' War that was about to be fought in America was just part of the larger international crisis that stemmed from the beginning of a new international phenomenon—the rise of the nation-state. The shift from the medieval order, based on local, organic government that was responsible to the spiritual powers and institutions, led to the modern concept of the nation, which claimed vast political powers and authority over the religious life of its subjects. This would result in the rise of nationalist movements in the German principalities, the Spanish kingdoms, the Italian kingdoms and city-states, and even in the long-united France.

Divorced from the transcendent, objective order of Christianity, these new states would adopt various ideologies as new religions of humanity to replace the old. Eventually, new systems of hedonistic morality would be exported to the colonies in the form of British government officials who intended to quench the flame of religious liberty and freedom that had been awakened by the religious revivals that had swept America.

DIVE DEEPER:
A PILGRIM'S PROGRESS

The great Victorian preacher, Charles Spurgeon, read it more than a hundred times. E.M. Bounds kept a copy by his bedside and read from it every night before retiring. Stonewall Jackson kept a copy in his knapsack throughout his Southern campaigns. D.L. Moody and Ira Sankey shared favorite passages from it each night before beginning their evangelistic services. C.S. Lewis believed it was "a literary and spiritual masterpiece." It is *Pilgrim's Progress*, a fanciful allegory of the Christian life, written primarily from a prison cell midway through the seventeenth century, by John Bunyan.

The son of a poor brazier, born in 1628, Bunyan was a witness to some of the momentous events in English history: the civil war, the regicide of King Charles, the Cromwell protectorate, the great fire, the restoration of the monarchy, and the great Puritan purge. Those were tumultuous days—days that left an indelible mark of change upon the souls of both men and nations. Bunyan was no exception. After a dramatic adult conversion, he immersed himself in the life and work of a very small non-conformist congregation.

After the demise of the protectorate and the subsequent restoration of the monarchy in 1660, persecutions were launched against all but established state churches. It was widely understood that religion was the primary influence on the nature and structure of culture. Preaching was considered to be a powerful force that had both eternal and temporal dimensions. Thus, they rightly predicted that a faithful exposition of the Bible would have immediate political and spiritual ramifications. Conservative Anglicans and Puritans thought that allowing unauthorized or unlearned men to preach would undermine the whole social fabric. They comprehended only too well the dynamic significance of worldviews.

For nearly a decade, Bunyan had served as an unordained, itinerant preacher and had frequently taken part in highly visible theological controversies. It was natural that the new governmental restrictions would focus on him. Thus, he was arrested for preaching to "unlawful assemblies and conventicles."

The judges who were assigned to his case were all ex-royalists, most of whom had suffered fines, sequestrations, and even imprisonments during the Interregnum. They threatened and cajoled Bunyan, but he was unshakable. Finally, in frustration, they told him they would not release him from custody until he was willing to forswear his illegal preaching. And so, he was sent to the county gaol where he spent twelve long years—recalcitrant to the end.

During his time in prison, he began writing the allegorical *Pilgrim's Progress* as a sort of spiritual autobiography. It describes his temptations, trials, and frustrations as well as his determination to risk all for the sake of spiritual integrity and the quest for righteousness.

Like *The Canterbury Tales*, *Don Quixote*, *The Aeneid*, and even *The Inferno*, the story is written as a travelogue—the hero embarks on a great adventure and must face many perils along the way until at long last he arrives at his destination or meets his destiny. In this case, brave Christian leaves his secure home in search of the Celestial City. Along the way he meets a vast array of characters, both good and evil, in an alternating landscape of dizzying deprivation and dazzling debauchery.

Around the rough framework of Christian's salvation and early discipleship is an episodic series of fearsome and fast-paced battles, discoveries, and encounters. He guides us through Puritan England's fairs, fields, and foibles, and he uncovers its competing psychologies, passions, and perplexities. But perhaps the liveliest and the most stimulating scenes in the story are the characterizations of the hypocrites and villains that Christian meets along the way. His loving, insightful, and exact observations of human nature are fiercely disarming and satirically precise. Bunyan's great universal appeal is his unerring genius in capturing the essence of everyday eccentricities.

Not surprisingly, *Pilgrim's Progress* is the best-selling religious book in American history, save the Bible—and it recurs time and again in the documentary narratives of America's earliest, most influential religious leaders. Much of that popularity has been manifested in our own day as so many believers begin to see themselves as pilgrims wandering in the wilderness of this poor, fallen world. Indeed, as John Crowe Ransom once asserted, "It may well be a more applicable parable for modernity than for any other period previous." Indeed, it may.

CHAPTER 4: THE EMERGENCE OF AN IMPERIAL ORDER

"Where tyranny begins, government ends."

The major powers in Europe, England and France, were growing weary of the constant state of warfare that began in 1689 and ran through King George's War. Unknown to the participants, new ideological shifts were occurring that would expand the parameters of the conflict on a scale unparalleled in human history. Countries began to adopt a nationalist philosophy, and this thinking combined with the rise of rationalism—the belief that man's powers of reason are sufficient apart from God's Word to understand and, more importantly, to control the material universe. The scientific theories of men like Francis Bacon and Galileo had at their roots a belief that the world ran on a series of mechanistic principles embedded in nature that operated independently from God. If man could use his reason to harness the power of these mechanistic principles, then humanity—and nations—could embark on a quest of unlimited progress completely apart from God.

The effect of rationalism was felt in many different areas of life. In religion, the result was Deism, which states that there is a Creator of the universe, but that after the creation, he left the world and never intervened. To sustain the mechanistic view of nature, God could never intrude; it had to be a completely enclosed system. There could be no supernatural events, meaning no miracles and no Holy Spirit. Since man's potential for progress rested with his reason, there was no recognition of man's sins, and since God could no longer intervene in history, and man no longer had to worry about the consequences of his sin, there was no need for Jesus. Thus, the idea of God was stripped from the relations of the three Persons of the Trinity to a bare and unknown Creator. In the colonies, the Unitarians represented this new, humanist religion, denying the Trinity and opposing the Great Awakening. Essentially, they denied that there could be any providential dealings of God in history. In America, this kind of thinking would be embraced by a number of prominent thinkers such as Ben Franklin, Thomas Jefferson, and Benjamin Rush.

There would also be a general decline in morality, since human conduct was no longer governed by divine commandments but the dictates of human reason. Whatever passions stirred in the heart of man received encouragement, because they reflected the order of nature. Because the Church of England was so closely tied to the political culture and its support drawn from tax revenues, it was used as a source of patronage for friends and relatives of the king and his ministers, which led to widespread corruption by those holding religious offices.

But the loss of biblical morality was not confined to the church. Back in England, social clubs were opened to serve the vices and natural impulses of the aristocratic elite, with some establishments, called "hell-fire" clubs, dedicated to blasphemous practices and perversity. Travelers from America, including Ben Franklin, indulged in all the pleasures that London society had to offer. British governors and other government officials, schooled in debauchery back home, would arrive in the New World to assume their offices and continue to conduct themselves in a manner that would regularly shock the frontier-hardened colonists.

Rationalism would also be applied to the economic realm, where these new ideas were active in the creation of a new kind of commercialism that stressed mass production and uniformity rather than individuality and craftsmanship. The resulting industrial age would draw workers from the farms and rural villages and crowd them into cities. But rather than lifting the peasants to improved social conditions and economic status, it would create a struggle against the trend of mechanized production, which left many without jobs and led to a new social phenomenon: urban unemployment.

INDUSTRIAL INNOVATION

It was not a time of bust for everyone. A new class of economic barons, such as Josiah Wedgewood, rode a wave of exponential growth in wealth and production under the protection of their friends in government. This relationship between the industrial princes and the ministers of state was a modern marriage of convenience of big business and government and would lead to a new approach of the old-world nations and their new-world colonies.

The American colonies were unique because they were more than trading outposts sending raw materials back to the home country; rather, they had developed industries and markets of their own. While they had been largely neglected by the British government in the 17th century due to a lack of interest and the internal political turmoil between the crown and Parliament, that was all about to change. The Hanoverian dynasty, beginning with George I, would give the English political structure stability as a compromise on the balance of power was achieved. The conflicts with France and the political settlement of the controversies between the Crown and Commons led to an increase of all things British. A culture of "Britannia" was promoted as a vehicle for expressing new nationalist sentiments, and the rallying call became "Make the world England!"

An imperial system, driven by the desire to create self-contained economic systems and reflecting the new national expectations, would take shape and dramatically change colonial policy in the 18th century. Rationalism would be combined with the new modes of commerce to create a type of economic nationalism called mercantilism. At the heart of this new philosophy was the attempt to use governmental power and policy to create wealth for a particular nation.

MERCANTILISM

There were characteristics common to the mercantilist systems instituted by the English, French, and Spanish. The primary motive was to obtain increasing amounts of gold and silver as a mark of the wealth of the nation. There were two means of accomplishing this—either by uncovering deposits in their new-world possessions or through trade. While the first source was declining as a means of revenue, trade policies would play a crucial role in maintaining the mercantilist system. Trade became tightly controlled as the governments tried to achieve "favorable balance of trade," meaning that they exported to the colonies and other countries more than they imported. This was achieved by preventing the colonies from trading directly with other countries, declaring prohibitions against developing raw materials into final products, royally granting monopolies in key industries and products, and imposing tariffs to make products from the colonies and foreign nations more costly than domestic products.

Despite the weariness of decades of conflict in Europe, war was the result of the protectionist policies of the respective countries. Each nation moved to secure their economic interests and advantages against the others, and this was played out in Europe, on the seas, and in the colonies around the globe on a scale unknown at the time. This directed attentions to the New World, where French and Spanish threats loomed on every side of the English colonies. The stage was set for the colossal clash of arms of the Seven Years' War, which Winston Churchill would call "the first world war."

UNFINISHED BUSINESS

The Treaty of Aix-la-Chapelle at the end of King George's War still left much conflict between French and English colonists unsettled. The French knew that by taking control of the Ohio River, they could link their American holdings between Quebec and New Orleans, thereby bottling up the English. In 1752,

Canada's governor, the Marquis Duquesne, ordered that a series of forts be built at strategic points in the region.

HIT THE ROAD, JACQUES

The English claimed the Ohio Valley region based on their colonial charters. In 1753, King George II ordered the colonial governors to tell any French trespassers to leave the Ohio Valley.

The first governor to take action was Governor Robert Dinwiddie of Virginia. Dinwiddie called into active duty a young twenty-two-year-old major in the Virginia militia named George Washington, who was sent to the western frontier with a polite message from the governor to the French commanders at Fort Venango and Fort Le Boeuf ordering them to leave. French commander Legardeur de St. Pierre refused in an equally polite manner.

WASHINGTON'S ADVANCE

George Washington turned out to be invaluable to Governor Dinwiddie. Not only did he display excellent diplomatic skills in his communications with the French and the Indians, but his experience as a surveyor also gave him a keen eye for strategic places in the region. He observed that a fort built at the Forks of the Ohio, where the Allegheny and Monongehela Rivers joined to form the Ohio River, could control all three bodies of water.

When Washington arrived back in Williamsburg on January 16, 1754, Governor Dinwiddie immediately dispatched Captain William Trent with a small contingent of men to begin constructing a fort at the Forks of the Ohio. The next month, Washington and a larger force were sent to join Trent's forces. Before they arrived, Trent's soldiers were attacked by French troops and had to withdraw. The French immediately began building Fort Duquesne.

WILDFIRE WAR

The French and Indian War was unlike previous colonial wars, which *began* in Europe and *spread* to America. This time it was the other way around; fighting began in Europe two years *after* hostilities commenced in America. The English colonists called the war on their end the French and Indian War, because that was who they were fighting, while the British referred to this conflict as the Seven Years' War or the Great War for Empire.

AND THEY'RE OFF

The French and Indian War began on May 28, 1754, when Washington's forces clashed with French armies at the Battle of Great Meadows. During the fray, the French commander and nine of his men were killed, and twenty-one others were captured by Washington's small force. Washington and his men hastily built Fort Necessity. When the French attacked, the English were forced to surrender, and Washington and his men were pushed out of the area. Their return to Virginia that summer left the French in full control of the Ohio Valley.

TAKING INVENTORY OF THE INFANTRY

At the outset of the war the French had many advantages. They had a well-trained army in America ready to fight, many strategically located forts in the disputed area, numerous Indian allies, and effective centralized leadership from the governor of New France.

Their primary weakness was that these troops were scattered and still outnumbered by the British fourteen to one.

English advantages included the most powerful navy in the world and a strong alliance with the Cherokee Indians in the south and the Iroquois in the north.

But the English colonists faced serious obstacles. The worst was that they lacked a centralized command. The colonies feared that too much power in the hands of one leader would result in tyranny. Most colonists were reluctant to lose blood and treasure unless they felt directly threatened. Those who lived in the safety of the seaboard cities felt that the frontiersmen were responsible for defending themselves.

FLINTLOCKS AND TOMAHAWKS

Meanwhile, far from the scene of the opening conflict, colonial delegates were holding a remarkable meeting in Albany, New York: the Albany Congress. Twenty-three colonial leaders, including Benjamin Franklin of Pennsylvania, sat down with 150 Iroquois chiefs to plan a common strategy against the French.

These Indians expressed doubt that the English could win this contest. One Mohawk leader bluntly stated, "You are desirous that we should open our minds, and our hearts to you; look at the French, they are men, they are fortifying everywhere but, we are ashamed to say it, you are all like women, bare and open without fortifications." Even when the delegates resorted to the time-honored way of sealing treaties with Indians—giving them many gifts—the Iroquois left without agreeing to help. As it turned out, they did eventually side with the English because of their long-standing hatred for the Indian allies of the French.

JOIN OR DIE

During the Albany Congress, Benjamin Franklin and six others forged a plan to enable the colonies to combine their manpower and resources to win this war. The Albany Plan of Union emphasized that the colonies must have unified organization to beat the French. The idea was to elect a president-general who would be paid by the king, and to assemble a Grand Council of forty-eight members to make laws. Council members would be chosen by the colonial legislatures and would deal with Indian affairs in the colonies and defense matters. The president-general would have the right to veto the Grand Council's laws, and the English king would be given final authority to approve or disapprove measures.

The biggest problem with the Albany Plan was that no one liked it. Both the colonies and the British crown thought the plan forced them to give up too much of their authority. They rejected the plan. A discouraged Benjamin Franklin accused all protesters of having "weak noodles."

BATTLE OF THE WILDERNESS

While all this debate was going on, news had traveled back to England that Washington's men had lost Fort Necessity. The English immediately dispatched General Edward Braddock to America in April of 1755 with an army of 1,400 English regulars, or professional soldiers. Joining him was a force of Virginia militia and the recently promoted lieutenant-colonel George Washington, who served as Braddock's aide-de-camp. Braddock's plan was simple: his force would carve a road through the wilderness to Fort Duquesne at the Forks of the Ohio.

Washington warned Braddock about the effective way the Indians and French fought in America. While Braddock was experienced fighting European-style, face to face in open country, the Indians hid behind trees and attacked by surprise. Braddock chose to ignore Washington's warnings. Eight miles from the Forks of the Ohio, a combined force of about 900 French, Canadians, and Indians assaulted the British army. They killed or wounded nearly a thousand of Braddock's troops. Braddock himself was shot in the lungs and died two days later. Washington had two horses shot out from under him and took four bullet holes in his coat. While he had not been able to persuade his commander to follow his wise advice, Washington did manage to turn a disastrous rout into an orderly retreat, leading the defeated band of survivors back to Virginia.

BLOWING HOLES
IN ENGLAND'S DEFENSE

After Braddock's Defeat of July 9, 1755, the English suffered one disaster after another. Finding the complete English war plans among Braddock's papers in the captured baggage train gave the French a tremendous advantage. They immediately began a series of savage raids on English frontier settlements from Pennsylvania to South Carolina.

The British war effort was also hindered by the Quakers in Pennsylvania. The civil government of that colony was still dominated by this pacifistic group, even though they were by now only a small percentage of Pennsylvania's population. The Quakers refused to participate in any military activity, not even to protect the settlers in the western part of their colony. The French and

Indians were definitely *not* pacifists and had no qualms about raiding English settlements. They destroyed houses and crops and slaughtered the settlers. After about two years of increasing carnage, non-Quaker Pennsylvanians such as Benjamin Franklin and others got together to do something about it. They pressured the Quakers to resign from civil government in 1756. A newly elected assembly voted to raise and equip a force to resist the attacks on their western settlements.

PITT TO ARMS

After three years of continual defeat, a new Prime Minister, William Pitt, took office in 1757. He replaced ineffective commanders, built up the navy, and sent an enormous army of 22,000 to America. Two aggressive young generals were dispatched to the colonies to head up the military effort—Jeffrey Amherst and James Wolfe.

By 1758, colonial soldiers aligned with English regulars to form a combined force of 50,000 men ready to fight. This strong English force then proceeded to capture the French Forts Louisbourg, Frontenac, Duquesne, Niagara, and Ticonderoga one by one.

MISSION IMPOSSIBLE?

The English were no longer satisfied with merely protecting their colonies, they wanted to capture all of New France as well. Generals Amherst and Wolfe joined forces to attack New France. The English strategy was to confront the French at two key cities in New France, Quebec and Montreal. Wolfe led a fleet into the St. Lawrence River toward Quebec, while Amherst marched an army through the Hudson River Valley toward Montreal.

The commander of the French army at Quebec, the Marquis de
Montcalm, felt sure that the city was safe because its position on a
high bluff would allow him to spot the English fleet coming from
miles away. However, Montcalm underestimated both the tenacity
and the craftiness of the English. On the night of September 12,
1759, Wolfe and 3,500 of his men left their ships for small boats
and paddled quietly with muffled oars up the St. Lawrence, right
past the French guards. They disembarked and marched toward
the city. At daybreak, Montcalm woke up to a nasty shock: the
British force stood ready to fight behind him on a level area called
the Plains of Abraham. In the ensuing battle, both Wolfe and
Montcalm lost their lives, but the English ultimately prevailed.
The Battle of Quebec sounded the death knell for the French empire in North America. The next year, the last French stronghold,
Montreal, surrendered to Amherst and his forces.

ADIEU, FRANCE!

The 1763 Treaty of Paris formally ended the Seven Years' War.
The English were the clear victors. France agreed to give England
all of New France as well as Louisiana east of the Mississippi River, except for the Isle of Orleans—the city of New Orleans. Britain
also received Florida from Spain. In return, the treaty awarded
Spain the portion of Louisiana west of the Mississippi. The only
areas remaining of the once mighty French Empire in America
were two rocky islands off the coast of Newfoundland, St. Pierre
and Miquelon, where French fishermen could clean and dry
their codfish. France's proud American Empire, over two and
half centuries old, had ended. Britain had emerged as the dominant power in North America.

There were significant ramifications for the colonies as a result of the British victory in the Seven Years' War. There was growing dissatisfaction at the long stream of incompetent and immoral governors and administrators sent by London to oversee the colonies. These positions, much like patronage system in the Church of England, were used for political payoffs and to occupy those aristocrats that had gone bankrupt back home or had become an embarrassment to the king. Incompetent governors were nothing new; in fact, it was common policy in the early part of the 1700s. Now, however, the stakes were much greater as England discarded its policy of salutary neglect and began to assert its claims and dominance over the colonies as part of its mercantilist policies.

The colonial assemblies had previously been able to control the governors by dictating their pay and limiting their discretion in spending public funds, but in the years immediately after the war, there would be growing resentment of the assemblies, as they no longer had to deal with just the inept and ineffectual colonial governors. Now they were under increasing assault by the Crown and Parliament.

This was a manifestation of a major shift in political philosophy in England. While the skirmishes in the 17th century occurred between the king and Parliament, which had the net effect of balancing the claims to power of each institution, the new political arrangement under the Hanoverian settlement fused together all of the power under a "King-in-Parliament" scheme. Instead of a divided government, the Crown worked directly with and through his cabinet and Prime Minister, who were members of Parliament. Rather than totally rejecting the divine right of kings doctrine, the English model asserted the same powers as the autocratic monarch in France, with the difference being that the English king worked more aggressively with the legislative branch of government.

The net effect of this new definition of political sovereignty was that the advancements in civil liberties achieved following the Glorious Revolution in 1688 were now subject to the larger interests of English mercantilism. The common law tradition became the victim of rationalism, and the rights that the colonists had enjoyed were being limited to bring the colonial assemblies under greater control of Parliament.

It is important to note that not everyone was unhappy with the newfound claims of the British government. Many American merchants benefited directly from the monopolies and tariff protections from foreign competitors. The war had ended the threat of invasion of the colonies by the French and pushed hostile Indian tribes further west into the frontier, just beyond the expanding settlements and villages that were springing up in every colony.

But the conflict had only masked the problems that were about to emerge as the newly-crowned King George III made plans to completely integrate the colonies into the new British Empire, even if this meant dramatically reversing the friendly taxation and trade policies the colonies had enjoyed up to that point. The war debts had mounted, and he felt that the colonies now needed to bear the full costs of their defense. His colonial governors would be instructed to extract those payments even if it required the use of the British troops that had been left in the colonies after the war.

The reaction of the colonists would vary. Many were still swept up with nationalistic fervor generated by the war effort and were grateful that the Roman Catholic threat from France had been vanquished. Others, however, were growing wary of the expansion of the claims of power by the British government. They remembered that they and their predecessors had fled from England to avoid the very absolutism that now replaced the French threat. They grew more troubled as the Church of England was used to advance the new political agenda. A new wave of persecutions directed at religious dissenters and clergy would be the first signs that a new order was being established in the colonies to force their submission to the new imperial order.

Religious, economic, political, and eventually, military conflicts would arise in the years ahead as they saw a shift in attitudes towards the colonists. While they were regarded as fellow British citizens possessing all the rights of their counterparts back in England as they fought in the colonial militias against the French, they would soon be seen as uncooperative colonial subjects opposing the "enlightened" policies of Crown and Commons. As the colonies felt the successive blows to their liberties and saw the corruption and indifference of the British governors and administrators, the resentment would light a wildfire that would bring America to a boiling point.

CHAPTER 5: TIGHTENING THE SCREWS

"No tyrant has ever effectually conquered and subjugated a people
whose liberties and public virtue were founded on the Word of God."

GARDINER SPRING

The coronation of King George III in October 1760 marked a turning point in the relations between England and her American colonies. His great-grandfather and grandfather, George I and George II, had allowed the powers of the Crown to decline under their rule. When he arrived from Hanover, George I, a native German, spoke no English, and the ministers of state had to speak to him in ecclesiastical Latin to conduct any conversation. George II was an absent king, spending most of his time back home in Hanover and leaving the administration of the country to his wife, Caroline, and his Prime Ministers, Sir Robert Walpole and William Pitt.

However, the new king was determined to be a new kind of English monarch, and a bold adjustment of style and policy was in order. Eager to assert his authority over his dominion, he began by dismissing many ministers of state that had been appointed by his grandfather, George II.

The most notable dismissal was William Pitt, the popular Prime Minister, who everyone acknowledged had been running the country during the entire course of the Seven Years' War. Pitt's departure from the government only served to increase the problems for the new king. The Peace of Paris, which ended the Seven Years' War, had left the British with the enormous problem of governing and protecting a new empire. On one side of the globe, they had added the subcontinent of India to their holdings; on the other, they had added Canada and all the land west of the Appalachians to the Mississippi River.

Victory in the war presented the king with a major defense headache. British North America more than doubled in size and now included many more hostile Indians and unfriendly Frenchmen. The king felt it necessary to station some 7,500 soldiers in the American colonies as a permanent defense against French and Indian raids along the frontier. Nearly half of the soldiers were earmarked for Canada, a quarter for duty in the West, almost a quarter for Florida, and seven hundred in the old colonial seaports to handle supplies destined for the soldiers on the frontier. The presence of these soldiers would prove to be a great source of trouble to the colonists, who did not believe that the British government should maintain a standing army in peacetime and grew suspicious that the intended purpose of these troops was to suppress their liberties.

PRINCETON V. THE PRINCE

Unknown to George at the time, a new kind of threat to his absolute authority as king was about to land on the American shores. John Witherspoon was a well-known preacher in Scotland who was called by the struggling College of New Jersey to assume the helm as president. The problem the college trustees were facing was that their presidents kept dying in rapid succession, including Jonathan Edwards and Samuel Davies, who both died just a few months into their terms. Little did the trustees know how good of a choice they had made in Witherspoon. Assessing the importance of Witherspoon's arrival to the colonies, Woodrow Wilson, who would himself serve as president of Princeton and then later be elected Governor of New Jersey and President of the United States, said, "It was a piece of providential good fortune that brought such a man to Princeton at such a good time."

Witherspoon, who had been imprisoned like so many other Scots patriots following the defeat of Bonnie Prince Charlie, quickly took to his new office, and he began to aggressively transform the college into a new kind of institution that was focused on creating cultural leaders. His biographer, Varnum Lansing Collins, noted the importance of this shift: "However little others may have thought of it or he himself have realized just then was the belief that the function of such a college was not merely to educate candidates for the ministry, but also to send out into the widening spheres of colonial life Christian gentlemen and scholarly men of affairs." The curriculum would now be devoted to more than just theology; it would prepare them for the whole of life.

Students would devote their time to learning "the permanent things", Witherspoon determined. New topics were incorporated into Witherspoon's moral philosophy lectures, including ethics, political science, and law—none of which were being taught at a college anywhere in the colonies at the time. Economics was also a part of the broadened academic focus, and he lectured against the use of paper money in favor of hard currency and the virtues of the free market.

These studies rooted the students in the Reformation doctrine of calling and vocation. Witherspoon emphasized the pervasive role of religion to guide and inform every area of study and the necessity of every man to do his duty, and he would echo this theme in a sermon delivered just days before he signed the Declaration of Independence: "Upon the whole, I beseech you to make a wise improvement of the present threatening aspect of public affairs, and to remember your duty to God, to your country, to your families, and to yourselves, is the same. True religion is nothing else but an inward temper and outward conduct suited to your state and circumstances in providence at any time."

Religion must be translated into action, and the whole education system at the College of New Jersey would be founded on this fundamental belief. Academics at the college were intended to build these "Christian gentlemen" who exhibited the traits of pragmatism, spiritual devotion, a love of liberty and virtue, and vigilance against tyranny and apathy. Witherspoon was dedicated to building a new, peculiar kind of man, and the impact of his efforts would profoundly influence the direction that the entire country was about to take by training a whole generation of American leaders and statesmen. Garry Wills, a modern historian, was not overstating his case when he said that

Witherspoon was "probably the most influential teacher in the history of American education."

KING'S COLLEGE V. THE KING

Across the Hudson River, a similar effort was taking place at King's College in New York. There a full-orbed classical curriculum was instituted with the intent of producing men of virtue committed to their civic duties. This project would produce two of the Founding era's leading statesmen, Alexander Hamilton and John Jay, who together with John Witherspoon's disciple, James Madison, would author the *Federalist Papers* during the later debates over ratifying the Constitution. These two colleges would be the most influential centers of learning in the years to come because of the unique philosophy and lifestyle, rooted in religious action, that they advocated.

This advancement of a uniquely Christian culture was important during this time because Deism and rationalism were beginning to take root in America. Circles of "enlightened" elite, representing the most influential people, were developing in many of the major cities in the colonies, particularly in Philadelphia, the third largest city in the British Empire. But unlike England, where depravity and religious skepticism ran rampant and unchecked, the American experience was a strange mixture of Enlightenment philosophy moderated by the influence of the Great Awakening.

This is why Ben Franklin, who fathered several illegitimate children, rejected orthodox Christianity, and indulged in the pleasures of London's "social clubs," could develop a close relationship with George Whitefield, leader of the Great Awakening revivals, and serve as the publisher of Whitefield's works. The two also discussed the establishment of a new colony dedicated to instituting and promoting distinctly Christian principles. This worldview confusion, born of the strong Christian influences in the colonies and combined with the explosion of wealth in the cities and the rise of rationalism, would account for the wide variety of responses to the new policies issued by King George back in London.

BOATLOADS OF DEBT

The enormous cost of fighting the French and Indian War had left England with a huge debt—more than 130 million pounds. This was the most important challenge faced by George Grenville, Prime Minister and First Lord of the British Treasury, when he took office in 1763. He was amazed to find out that his customs service in America actually cost four times what it collected in duties. Americans regularly imported molasses from the French West Indies and were supposed to be paying six pence per gallon import duty. Alarmed that this duty was largely being ignored, Grenville ordered the British navy to immediately begin enforcing it.

Grenville was also irritated with the colonies for trying to deal with their chronic currency shortage by issuing their own paper money. The amount in circulation was small, but it was worth less than gold or silver English coin. Many English merchants feared that American customers might try to pay their debts with this paper money. Back in 1751, the New England colonies had been forbidden from making paper money legal tender. This meant that it could not be used to pay debts or taxes of any sort. Grenville's Currency Act of 1764 applied this law to all of the American colonies.

At the same time, Parliament passed the Revenue Act of 1764, better known as the Sugar Act, which reduced the molasses tax from six pence to three pence per gallon and put new duties on sugar, indigo, coffee, pimento, wine, and textiles. Because colonial smugglers were nearly always acquitted by colonial juries, an important provision of this law said that those accused of violating these customs regulations would have to be tried in British admiralty courts. Judges in these courts were appointed directly by the king and made their decisions without juries. Taking away the accused smuggler's right to a jury trial was a serious departure from English custom. Added to that was the fact that the Sugar Act was the first law ever passed by Parliament for the specific purpose of raising revenue (tax money) in the colonies to help pay for the government's expenses.

While the colonists were alarmed at the Sugar Act, the Stamp Act, which parliament passed in 1765 on Grenville's recommendation, roused them to even greater anger. This law stated that legal documents, newspapers, diplomas, playing cards, and all published matter could only be printed on stamped paper which had to be bought from tax officials. The "stamp" was not a stamp as we know it, but was an embossed imprint on the paper that certified that the tax had been paid. The Stamp Act also provided that violators could be tried without a jury in the admiralty courts. Some members of Parliament objected and predicted that American colonists would not pay the new taxes. It passed anyway and was signed by the king in April of 1765.

To make matters worse, in May of 1765, Grenville introduced the Quartering Act. Though it required only that *unoccupied* buildings be made available for the soldiers' lodging, some colonists remembered how British troops occupying Scotland and Ireland many years earlier had moved into *occupied* private dwellings and had caused much suffering and resentment.

MAGNA MESS

Grenville's program sent waves of shock and anger from Georgia to Massachusetts. Colonists feared that Grenville was determined to strip the Americans of their rights as English citizens. Never before had they been taxed, except by their elected colonial representatives. Until now, they had all enjoyed the fundamental right of trial by a jury chosen from their fellow citizens as guaranteed by the Magna Carta. And now Grenville was making plans to station British troops permanently in their midst. With the French driven from North America and the Indians no longer a major problem, many wondered why such troops were needed—unless this was all part of a conspiracy to take away their rights by force.

This escalation of hostilities between America and England would move several new leaders and movements to center stage in colonial politics. In Virginia, a young attorney name Patrick Henry would rally the divided House of Burgesses to oppose the Stamp Act. He authored a series of resolutions that were narrowly approved by the assembly protesting the new legislation. The resolutions affirmed the right of the colonies to govern themselves and challenged the power of the Parliament to institute the new levies, warning that these measures were direct threats to their liberties as Englishmen. One asserted that "the General Assembly of this colony have the only sole and exclusive right and power to lay taxes [...] upon the inhabitants of this colony, and that every attempt to vest such power in any person or persons whatsoever [...] has a manifest tendency to destroy British as well as American freedom."

This was not the first time that Patrick Henry came to the attention of British authorities. He began his career as a lawyer by assisting dissenting pastors who were charged with preaching without a license. His interest in religious liberties began when he was a boy and he would accompany his mother and grandfather, both ardent dissenters, to hear Samuel Davies, who ministered at a church in nearby Hanover. Henry would listen intently to Davies' thundering style and watch his emotional gestures, which he would later adopt in his legal argumentation.

Henry would first come to public attention in the celebrated case of the Parson's Cause, where a member of the Anglican clergy, James Maury, sued for back pay of tobacco. Since he was a member of the established church, he was entitled to the equivalent of sixteen thousand pounds of tobacco, worth about 400 pounds sterling, each year that was to be collected as part of the tax revenue by government agents. In 1758, a drought pushed up the price of tobacco and the legislature forced the clergy to accept paper money instead of sterling at the price of two penny per pound, cutting their salary by almost a third. In 1763, Maury sued, claiming that he was due the full amount under law. At the trial, he won, and a date was appointed for a jury to decide what damages were due to the ministers.

The defendant, Thomas Johnson, was one of the richest men in the colony and was desperate for an attorney to represent him in the hearing, and he turned to Patrick Henry, who had just recently taken up the law. Peter Lyons, one of the most distinguished attorneys in the area, was representing Maury, and Henry was troubled that his father, Colonel John Henry, was serving as the judge in the case. But his spirits were bolstered when he saw that the jury included several members of dissenting churches and his own cousin. In his argument, he railed against the unpopular establishment church and accused the Anglican ministers of taking food and clothes from the poorest citizens. He reminded the jury that they were not required to award Maury anything, but if they did, it should be nothing more than a token. The jury left and immediately returned, where they delivered their verdict of the award to Rev. Maury—one penny. Henry was swept out of the courtroom on the shoulders of the jubilant crowd that had gathered to hear the case, and his fame from the Parson's Cause would bring him many new wealthy clients and catapult him into the House of Burgesses, where he would gain even more notoriety for his opposition of the Stamp Act.

COLONIAL REPRESENTATION

In Massachusetts, an effort, really a movement, was started, suggesting that all the colonies send representatives to a meeting that would coordinate a combined colonial resistance to parliamentary taxation. Nine of the thirteen colonies sent representatives to the Stamp Act Congress, which met in New York City in October of 1765. Pledging their loyalty to the crown, they insisted that admiralty courts and taxation for revenue were wrongful exercises of Parliament's authority. George III and Parliament were sent petitions asking that the Sugar Act and Stamp Act be repealed.

Perhaps the most effective action taken as a result of the Stamp Act Congress was the agreement among the merchants of New York, Philadelphia, and Boston to boycott British goods. This, they hoped, would put pressure on British merchants selling in America to bring pressure on Parliament to repeal the Stamp Act. A secret organization called the Sons of Liberty was formed by Americans impatient with simply waiting and hoping that Parliament might back down. Their members intimidated some stamp agents into resigning, tarred and feathered others, and organized mobs, which effectively prevented the Act from going into effect on November 1.

Grenville had no chance to respond to events across the Atlantic since King George III had fired him in July for political reasons of his own and replaced him with the Marquis of Rockingham. Rockingham and his followers had originally opposed the Stamp Act, so he asked Parliament to repeal it. English merchants who had lost hundreds of thousands of pounds of American business enthusiastically supported this move.

Parliament, however, was reluctant to back down in the face of American resistance, which had included mob action. Nevertheless, Parliament did repeal the Stamp Act in March of 1766, but only after passing the Declaratory Act. This law said that Parliament had the right to legislate for the colonies "in all cases whatsoever." Americans were so delighted over the repeal of the Stamp Act that they barely noticed the Declaratory Act, at least for a while.

THEN CAME TOWNSHEND

England regained the attention of the colonies later that year as
they considered retaliatory actions against the Americans. The
opportunity for the Crown to strike came after George III replaced the Marquis of Rockingham, who had seemed to be a real
friend to the colonists, with William Pitt, now the Earl of Cha-
tham. Poor health prevented the brilliant Pitt from governing effectively. His Chancellor of the Exchequer, Charles Townshend,
assumed the most influential role in the new government. One
of Townshend's first acts was to persuade Parliament to pass the
Townshend Duties, which put new taxes on all glass, paint, paper, lead, and tea that America imported from England.

A letter of protest was drafted by the Massachusetts assembly and immediately circulated around the colonies. Virginia,
South Carolina, New Hampshire, New Jersey, and Connecticut responded with enthusiastic agreement. When the British
government ordered the Massachusetts legislature to rescind
this circular letter because it showed a "dangerous and factious
tendency," the representatives refused by a vote of ninety-two to
seventeen. The British responded by transferring two regiments
of soldiers from Nova Scotia to Massachusetts. They arrived in
Boston aboard warships on September 28, 1768.

George Washington and Patrick Henry led Virginia's resistance to the Townshend Duties. There the House of Burgesses
passed resolutions affirming their right to petition the crown
and denying that Parliament had the right to tax the colonies.
The success of the boycott of British goods in response to the
Stamp Act led American merchants to once again make a non-
importation agreement. The effectiveness of this measure can be

seen in the fact that colonial imports declined from £2,378,000 in 1768 to £1,634,000 in 1769. The bill, which Townshend had assured Parliament would raise £40,000 per year in America, yielded only £16,000 in *three* years, and it cost the British authorities £200,000 to collect it.

UNTRUE NORTH

When Townshend died in 1767 at the age of forty-one, the king appointed Lord North to take his place. North immediately recommended that all of the Townshend Duties be repealed except the tax on tea. He was willing to compromise on nearly everything except the authority of Parliament. He believed that since the colonies had to import all of their tea and could not produce it at home, they would be willing to pay this small tax. Besides, this tax would maintain the principle of Parliament's supremacy over the colonies, which was laid down in the Declaratory Act. Most Americans greeted the news of the repeal of the Townshend duties with enthusiasm and ended their boycott of British goods.

MASSACRE IN MASSACHUSETTS

The arrival of British troops in Boston caused some Americans to wonder whether there was a deliberate plot by the crown to take away their rights as Englishmen. The haughtiness of the soldiers added to Bostonians' resentment of them. Antagonism between citizens and soldiers escalated during the fall of 1769. "Lobsterback" became one of the milder insults shouted at soldiers marching off to guard duty.

In October, angry protesters attacked one detachment of troops, though the soldiers kept their composure and no shots were fired. Protests continued during the winter. The soldiers were "too few to preserve order, yet numerous enough to goad the patriots and remind them of military despotism."

Finally, on the snowy night of March 5, 1770, irate dockworkers came upon a British soldier standing guard and pelted him with insults, snowballs, and rocks. About twenty soldiers came to his aid, while the angry mob grew to two hundred. The British ordered the crowd to disperse. They refused. Captain Preston, in charge of the troops, tried to reason with the mob. He failed. Preston ordered the soldiers *not* to fire. Unfortunately, one was hit by a club and fired his musket. The other soldiers heard that shot and returned fire. When the smoke cleared, five Bostonians lay dead and several more were wounded.

The tensions in the colonies had finally come to bloodshed, and the course of the conflict between England and the Americans had reached a watershed. The years since the end of the Seven Years' War had seen repeated attempts by Parliament to defend their economic grip on the colonies, and the colonial assemblies had replied with protests and boycotts. They grew suspicious that plans had been made to subvert their long-held liberties. Now the British required troops to enforce their edicts and had spilt American blood.

This escalation of hostilities by King George's government confirmed the worst fears of the radical forces that had to date been localized and kept to the margins of the conflict. But the Boston Massacre gave them vindication and shifted large numbers of supporters to their side. While groups like the Sons of Liberty in Boston and the Philadelphia Society in Pennsylvania were small in number, their voices were amplified by this profound tragedy.

The colonial printing presses would run virtually non-stop over the next few years as discontent and dissatisfaction boiled over into hatred and rebellion.

Parliament would add fuel to the fire with new measures to assert their dominance by limiting the powers of the colonial assemblies. They would also dispatch more of the hated British troops to America, igniting the fires of resistance up and down the Atlantic Coast. And now that the colonies had established relations with each other and actively communicated about tactics and formulating a coordinated response, their power and effectiveness would increase. As the smoke from the Boston Massacre cleared, a radicalized and unified opposition by the colonists would begin to take shape.

DIVE DEEPER: AS A MAN THINKETH

The students in America's earliest schools, academies, and colleges were educated according to the great traditions of the Christian classical heritage. They were the beneficiaries of a rich legacy of art, music, and ideas that not only trained the extraordinary minds of our Founding Fathers, but also had promoted the remarkable flowering of culture throughout western civilization. It was a pattern of academic discipleship that had hardly changed at all since the dawning days of the Reformation and Renaissance—a pattern that has almost entirely vanished today.

Indeed, those first colonial Americans were educated in a way that we can only dream of today, despite all our nifty gadgets, gimmicks, and bright ideas. They were steeped in the ethos of Augustine, Dante, Plutarch, and Vasari. They were conversant in the ideas of Seneca, Ptolemy, Virgil, and Aristophanes. The notions of Athanasius, Chrysostom, Anselm, Bonaventure, Aquinas, Machiavelli, Abelard, and Wycliffe informed their thinking and shaped their worldview.

The now carelessly discarded traditional medieval Trivium—emphasizing the basic classical scholastic categories of grammar, logic, and rhetoric—equipped them with the tools for a lifetime of learning: a working knowledge of the timetables of history, a background understanding of the great literary classics, a structural competency in Greek and Latin-based grammars, a familiarity with the sweep of art, music, and ideas, a grasp of research and writing skills, a worldview comprehension of math and science basics, a principled approach to current events, and an emphasis on a Christian life paradigm.

The methodologies of this kind of classical learning adhered to the time-honored principles of creative learning: an emphasis on structural memorization, an exposure to the best of Christendom's cultural ethos, a wide array of focused reading, an opportunity for disciplined presentations, an experience with basic academic skills, and a catechizing for orthopraxy as well as orthodoxy.

The object of this kind of classical education was not merely the accumulation of knowledge. Instead, it was to equip a whole new generation of leaders with the necessary tools to exercise discernment, discretion, and discipline in their lives and over their callings. Despite their meager resources, rough-hewn facilities, and down-to-earth, frontier ethic, they maintained continuity with all that had given birth to the wisdom of the west.

It was the modern abandonment of these classical standards generations later that provoked G.K. Chesterton to remark:

> The great intellectual tradition that comes down to us from the past was never interrupted or lost through such trifles as the sack of Rome, the triumph of Attila, or all the barbarian invasions of the Dark Ages. It was

lost after ... the coming of the marvels of technology, the establishment of universal education, and all the enlightenment of the modern world. And thus was lost—or impatiently snapped—the long thin delicate thread that had descended from distant antiquity; the thread of that unusual human hobby: the habit of thinking.

CHAPTER 6: REBELLION BREWING

"Religious liberty is so blended with civil, that if one falls it is not expected that the other will continue."

CHARLES TURNER

The wave of patriotic sentiment that swept the colonies during the Seven Years' War had suddenly given way to a climate of resentment and distrust. Unfavorable taxation and trade policies were being implemented and the English troops that had been left in America after the Seven Years' War, under the pretense of defending the colonies from any remaining French and Indian threats, were now being used as part of the Crown's domestic policy to bring the colonies into subjection. This caused a rapid escalation in hostilities between the people of Boston and the British soldiers now stationed there. And now shock and dismay began to set in as the citizens attempted to deal with the events of the Boston Massacre.

Thousands of mourners flooded Boston as the city buried the victims of the massacre. Even in the days immediately following the shootings, all observers concluded that the situation had changed dramatically. The unthinkable had just occurred, and many of the wealthy and religious citizens of Boston that had remained indifferent to the growing conflicts between the colonial radicals and British officials now lined up solidly behind the militants. Extreme events now called for extreme measures, and the man that many in Boston looked to in the days following the tragedy was Samuel Adams.

THE BOSTON BREWER

Sam Adams was recognized as Boston's leading antagonist and opponent to British policy and presence. A spiritually devout man, he had been significantly influenced by George Whitefield's preaching while he was a student at Harvard and seriously considered entering the clergy. His senior thesis anticipated his radical politics, arguing that even the highest lawful authorities could be resisted when the powers of the government threatened the safety and liberties of the commonwealth. At his father's death, he inherited the family malt business, but his passion was politics.

A master political strategist, he utilized the powers of communications and propaganda to shape public opinion. In the 1750s, he and a group of friends formed a secret society and began publishing the *Independent Advertiser*, by which they attacked the British government's policies and appointed officials. He would later learn much from his mentor, James Otis, a Boston attorney that was one of the few voices opposing the expansion of governmental powers and the increasing use of writs of assistance.

These legal documents granted customs officials broad and un-defined authority to search and confiscate property under the guise of looking for smugglers who conducted business around the Boston harbor. Otis would be a regular contributor to the cause, including the publication of his 1764 tract, *Rights of Colonies Asserted and Proved*, which argued in response to the Sugar Act that the Parliament had no right to tax the colonies. But his wild mood swings made him unpredictable, and most turned to Adams for leadership.

The leadership abilities of Sam Adams were not confined to his writings; he was the consummate people person. He could as easily talk with the dockworker at the harbor as he could with members of the elite of Boston society. He was well-respected because he took his Congregationalist religion seriously, and in his job as tax collector, he gained many friends by his lax enforcement during times of economic hardship. With an ability to craft a message, formulate a political strategy, and then mobilize the forces to make it happen, Sam Adams was feared by the British and respected by the masses.

UNDER LIBERTY'S TREE

Adams' greatest success in his early days as an activist was the creation of the Sons of Liberty. This organization served on the front lines of the cause of liberty in Boston, and their success in forcing the British to consistently reverse their policies prompted other secret societies around New England to adopt their strategies. The Sons of Liberty were able to translate their popularity into momentum to obtain seats in the Massachusetts House and take control of the Boston Town Meeting.

It was after the passage of the Stamp Act that the Sons of Liberty first showed their muscle. Staging regular demonstrations in Boston around the "Liberty Tree," they were also behind the coordinated campaigns to pressure colonial citizens not to accept positions as Stamp agents. Riots would regularly be directed against those that resisted, and several agents reluctant to resign their commissions had their houses and offices torn down. When the crowds would overstep their bounds, Adams would immediately denounce the riots and distance himself from their actions, but few doubted who controlled the mobs.

The Sons of Liberty also pushed for the Stamp Act Congress, which gave the activists connections with the political leaders in the other colonies. They also coordinated with other like-minded groups in the area, such as the Loyal Nine, a group of merchants dedicated to preserving the freedom of the colony. After Lord North moved British soldiers into Boston, Adams set up a news service, *Journal of the Times*, to recap supposed abuses committed by the soldiers against the populace, which was frequently laced with some suggestive and unflattering storytelling. Another active member of the Sons of Liberty was the silversmith Paul Revere. After the Boston Massacre, Revere would make an engraving commemorating the event, which would spread his name up and down the Atlantic seaboard.

One additional success the Sons of Liberty enjoyed was the campaign against Boston merchants that purchased and sold goods imported from England. Their hope was to turn the mercantilist system against the mother country by denying them the business they needed to achieve favorable balance of trade. They organized effective boycotts against uncooperative merchants, so much so that even the acting Massachusetts governor, Thomas Hutchinson, and his sons refused to violate the Sons of Liberty's embargoes.

GENTLEMAN JOHN

One of the prime beneficiaries of the non-importation agreements was the Boston merchant, John Hancock. Inheriting the family business from his uncle and now one of the richest men in the colonies, Hancock ran a booming trading business that relied on smuggling products into America. He frequently ran afoul of the British customs agents, and as early as 1768, he was refusing to pay customs for the goods on his ships. Even though Hancock had been defeated by Sam Adams for a seat in the colonial assembly, he would later win another seat and become a close friend and partner with Adams. His deep pockets would come in handy for the struggling movement. His role in the anti-government circles led John Witherspoon to grant him an honorary degree from the College of New Jersey in 1769, more for his political activities than his depth of knowledge.

PENMAN OF THE REVOLUTION

Another recipient of one of Witherspoon's honorary degrees that year was John Dickinson, a prominent leader of the colonial resistance in Pennsylvania. His series of anonymous letters, published by a "Pennsylvania Farmer," during the Townshend Acts crisis warned of the extreme danger to liberty from allowing Parliamentary taxation to be recognized in America. One early American historian, David Ramsey, writing in 1789, said of Dickinson's letters that "their reasoning was so convincing, that many of the candid and disinterested citizens of Great Britain, acknowledged that the American opposition to parliamentary taxation was justifiable." Such was the power of his pen, which would be used time and again as the new country took shape.

THE PEN AND THE SWORD

Despite the repeal of the Townshend Duties and the easing of tensions in Boston, Samuel Adams and other Sons of Liberty stayed busy. In 1772, Adams persuaded Massachusetts towns to put into writing their grievances against Great Britain and statements of American rights and to regularly correspond with each other on such matters. The other New England colonies soon followed suit. The Virginia assembly led the way in the South by setting up a committee of correspondence for the entire colony and suggested that all the other colonies do the same. These Committees of Correspondence were important. They became a way of reporting and sharing news outside of the regular newspapers. They could also be used as a means for the colonies to take common stands on issues and to act together on such matters as they thought necessary. This coordination between colonies would be crucial in making appeals to King George in response to the policies imposed by his ministers. As soon as new taxes and schemes were devised, the colonies would have a formal reply at the ready.

NEW TENSIONS

As passions subsided after the Boston Massacre, the colonial resistance would see some gains and setbacks. The event forever altered the political landscape, and the effects would be felt for several years afterwards. The trial of the soldiers involved in the shootings were found not guilty by a Massachusetts jury in December 1770, which made many feel that justice was not served. It didn't help that a cousin of Sam Adams, John Adams, had served as a defense attorney for the group.

Tensions between the colonists and the British government continued over the next few years. Tempers would flare and then subside. But it was clear that a new radicalism was emerging. The first sign of trouble was when a group of colonists burned a British ship in Rhode Island that had been harassing traders and stopping small boats headed for market. The *Gaspee* was assigned to patrol Narragansett Bay to catch smugglers, and in June 1772, it went after a ship suspected of carrying illegal goods. When the ship ran aground, word quickly spread around Newport, and a group of men rowed out to the *Gaspee* and took control of the ship. Allowing the crew to gather their belongings, everyone was ordered off the ship, and the ship was set afire, never to disrupt the smugglers again. Despite an official investigation, no one was ever arrested or tried in the matter.

TEA TIME

The British would find a new cause for alarm in a familiar place: Boston. Lord North had recommended that Parliament pass the Tea Act of 1773. This was passed not so much to regulate trade or even to make money, but mainly to help the British East India Company get out of financial trouble. This law allowed the company to export tea directly from India to America without requiring it to be unloaded in England first. This would cut the company's costs considerably. The tea would still have a small tax of three pence per pound on it, but it would be sold in the colonies at a price lower than one could buy it for in England. King George III had insisted on this tax in order to uphold Parliament's right to tax the colonies. Even with this tax, Americans would pay less for British tea than they were paying for tea smuggled from Holland.

Both the king and Lord North failed to understand the American position. Americans were not willing to pay *any* tax levied by Parliament, no matter how small it might be. It would also put smugglers, like John Hancock, out of business because the Dutch tea that they sold would not be able to compete with the new British monopoly. The arrival of the East India tea in American ports was met with fierce and determined resistance. Charleston port officials seized the tea, kept it in the customhouse, and later sold it. New York and Philadelphia refused entry to the tea-laden ships. When Governor Hutchinson of Massachusetts refused a petition to send the tea ships back to England, a group of the Sons of Liberty disguised as Mohawk Indians boarded the ships on the night of December 16, 1773 and dumped 342 chests of tea into the harbor. Not one participant in this Boston Tea Party took any tea with him, nor did he destroy any property except for the tea itself. They even replaced the locks on the tea chests after they had emptied them. Hutchinson was furious—his sons and friends held the Massachusetts monopoly for the East India tea. He was soon writing to London asking for drastic action.

THE BRITISH REVOLUTION

The calls by the colonial governors for retaliation would soon be answered. A new set of punitive regulations, which the colonists called the "Intolerable Acts," were about to be imposed that would drive the wedge between America and England even deeper.

But another struggle was taking place back in England between two competing approaches to government, which like the Seven Years' War, would partially be played out in America. The old rivalry between limited, constitutional government and the autocratic divine right of kings had divided England in the 17th century between King and Parliament. These two opposing institutions would fight back and forth for an entire century until the time of King George III.

George wanted to be a new kind of king, but in the end, he became all too much like the older ones. He saw that Parliament could be brought together under his control by using his power to appoint Cabinet ministers and supporting his favorites in the parliamentary elections. Those he could not elect himself he would buy off with privileges and titles. The result was that the division of powers, a system hailed by such political thinkers as Baron de Montesquieu and John Locke, was united into a centralized whole under the domination of the king. All of the political advancements achieved by the English Civil War and the Glorious Revolution were wiped away: rather than having a divine right of kings, England would live under the divine right of Parliament, which was now under control of the king.

This new form of government had opponents and defenders. One of the primary critics of this new system in Parliament was Edmund Burke. He would become the most vocal ally of the colonies in the days ahead, and he regularly challenged the newfound powers of the Crown. He opposed the use of arbitrary power and believed that human nature was corrupt, which led him to oppose George's—and Parliament's—exercise of absolute power.

One apologist for the British Revolution in government was Sir William Blackstone, a British jurist who wrote the most influential legal textbook in history, the *Commentaries on the Laws of England*. Published in both England and America during this period, Blackstone was widely cited by both sides of the conflict in America as support for each position. But he clearly advocated Parliamentary sovereignty—the belief that absolute power resided there and that it could act in whatever manner it chose. And he rejected the view that the colonists were entitled to the same rights as those citizens still living in England. In an odd twist, Blackstone's *Commentaries* were well received in America because it presented the law in a coherent and systematic format for the first time ever, and they would sell better and be reprinted more often here than in England.

The limitation of the rights of the colonists was a real concern. At the beginning of the reign of George III, American lawyers were fighting the issuance of writs of assistance, which granted unlimited power of search and seizure to tax collectors and customs officials. New abuses were looming on the horizon, and the colonists would vigorously protest being denied the rights they had always enjoyed and the changing attitude towards the colonies. Politicians and the populace back in Mother Britain no longer saw their American cousins as an extension of England, but as conquered territories subject to whatever tax or trade measures that Parliament deemed appropriate.

The Boston Tea Party was as much of an attack on this new vision of government as it was about protecting the traders and merchants who provided the colonies with their tea. The money collected from the new tax was going to be used to pay the salaries of the colonial governors, removing the authority and limitations on power that the colonial assemblies had maintained since they were founded by the first settlers. The new British territories acquired in Canada would not have representative assemblies but would be governed directly from London. Colonists feared that their assemblies could be shut down, and the end run that Parliament was attempting by paying the governors' salaries with taxes collected by British government officials gave them good reason to be troubled.

REFORMATION OR REVOLUTION?

Two visions were in direct conflict: would society be governed from the bottom-up, with an organic, limited system of government, or would the state assume total control and rule from the top-down? The British Empire now claimed absolute power and was attempting to conduct a complete revolution to bring everything in its dominions under this new regime. This was in opposition to the growth and government of the colonies up until this time, and much of the struggle between England and America was rooted in the reluctance of the colonists to concede their rights and way of life. They enjoyed relatively broad religious, economic, and political freedoms, and they believed that these rights were given by God and not subject to alteration by Parliament.

More and more, the colonists felt as though something had to be done against this encroachment on their rights. The Boston Tea Party gave the radicals a symbolic victory, but it was not going to stop the English from trying again. As England tried to tighten its grip on the colonies, many questions would arise. How far could the colonies resist? If it came to the point of armed conflict, when would they know the moment that such action was required? Would the colonies stand together or fall apart? Few were eager to take on the greatest military power in the world, but the events of the next few years would force the colonial leaders to weigh these questions as British Redcoats arrived in America more frequently to quash the brewing rebellion. As the threat to liberty increased, many of these leaders would reluctantly consider a response that would be considered treason by the English. The stakes were being raised, and it was becoming clear to the colonists that the choice was going to be freedom or slavery.

CHAPTER 7: RELUCTANT REVOLUTIONARIES

"Is life so dear, or peace so sweet, as to be purchased at the price of chains and slavery? Forbid it, Almighty God! I know not what course others may take, but as for me: give me liberty or give me death!"

PATRICK HENRY

As the English tea heaved off the newly-arrived ships settled at the bottom of Boston Harbor, news of the Boston Tea Party electrified the colonies. At the College of New Jersey, students staged their own "tea party" with whatever tea they could find in the area. In South Carolina, William Tennent III, pastor of the Independent Church of Charleston, wrote an open letter to the ladies of the community asking for their cooperation in the boycott on English tea. Struck by the boldness of the momentous events in Boston, everywhere was abuzz with the news.

The leaders of the event had calculated a shrewd strategy: with careful planning and staging of the raid, they were able to avoid the charge of anarchy. But regardless, the leaders of the Sons of Liberty anticipated a response from the British. Such a daring move against the government's policy was certain to have ramifications.

DUMPED TEA DEMANDS DISCIPLINE

Lord North was convinced that Boston was the center of the rebellion infecting all the other colonies, so he decided to make an example of the city. At his suggestion, Parliament passed four laws which they called the Coercive Acts, but which the Americans were soon calling the Intolerable Acts. The Boston Port Act closed the port of this seafaring city until Bostonians paid for the destroyed tea. The Massachusetts Government Act made changes which put the colonial government directly under the king. The Quartering Act made it easier to station troops in privately-owned buildings when their commander thought it a military necessity. The Administration of Justice Act said that any British official accused of a serious crime would be tried in England instead of in the colony. The British felt that colonial officials could not receive a fair trial before colonial juries, but the Americans believed that British juries would acquit the officials, no matter how horrid the crime. As a result, they called the Administration of Justice Act the "Murder Act." Finally, the British fired Massachusetts Governor Hutchinson and replaced him with General Thomas Gage, who was also the commander-in-chief of all the British troops in North America. The colonists immediately recalled the tyranny back in the 1680s, when another military man, Sir Edmund Andros, had been made governor of all New England, and saw in Gage's appointment yet more evidence of a growing British assault on their colonial liberties.

Shortly after passing the Coercive Acts, Parliament passed the Quebec Act. This bill was aimed primarily at the Canadian province of Quebec, recently acquired by the British in the French and Indian War. It provided for freedom of worship for the majority of Roman Catholics in that province. It also set up a government that did not include a representative assembly. The colonists wondered why an English colony would be governed without a representative assembly—something entirely new to their experience—and they were even more upset that the Quebec Act redrew the boundaries of that colony to include all the area west of the Appalachian Mountains and southward from Quebec to the Ohio River. The Quebec Act was lumped together with the Coercive Acts in the minds of the colonists who began referring to the act as merely another one of the Intolerable Acts.

The Committees of Correspondence immediately began to sound the alarm throughout the colonies over these developments. The influence these groups had can be seen in the outpouring of sympathy and gifts to Boston. Pennsylvania sent flour and the Carolinas sent rice to help the beleaguered city. Virginia's House of Burgesses declared a day of fasting and prayer to coincide with the day that the Intolerable Acts were to go into force. When the royal governor dismissed them for their action, they left the House and reassembled in Williamsburg's Raleigh Tavern. There they proposed that delegates from all the colonies ought to meet annually, a suggestion that was to have a far-reaching impact.

THE FIRST CONTINENTAL CONGRESS

After the Port Act of March 1774 closed its seaport, Boston sent a circular letter to all the colonies calling for a complete boycott of all trade between Britain and America. The response was not encouraging. Philadelphia and New York, however, did call for a general congress to discuss the problems of the colonies. The Massachusetts legislature gave up its plan for a boycott and in June sent out another circular letter requesting a meeting of delegates from the colonial Committees of Correspondence. By the end of August, delegates from all the colonies but Georgia began drifting into Philadelphia.

Fifty-five leaders from twelve colonies gathered in Carpenter's Hall in Philadelphia on September 5, 1774 to form the First Continental Congress. The delegates selected as their first chairman Peyton Randolph of Virginia. They then agreed to call their assemblage "The Congress" and the chairman "The President." Thus, Peyton Randolph, not George Washington, was in fact the true first "President of the United States." Charles Thomson, known as "the Sam Adams of Philadelphia," was elected secretary, a post he held until the new United States Constitution abolished the Continental Congress in 1788.

One of the first orders of business was to read the instructions from the home "governments" charging the delegates "to consult on the present state of the colonies [...] and to deliberate and determine upon wise and proper measures [...] for the recovery and establishment of their just rights and liberties [...] and the restoration of union and harmony between Great Britain and the colonies [...]." The Congress was not given the power to make laws or to govern, but only to consult and discuss. After

hearing their instructions, the delegates entered into a long discussion over voting procedure. Representatives from the larger
colonies wanted representation in proportion to the population,
but representatives from the smaller colonies feared that they
would be dominated by the larger colonies. The lack of any reliable population statistics aided the cause of the smaller colonies,
and in the end, the delegates decided that each colony would get
one vote, regardless of its size. It was during this debate that Patrick Henry of Virginia remarked, "Government is dissolved....
We are in a state of nature, sir. The distinctions between Virginians, Pennsylvanians, New Yorkers, and New Englanders, are no
more. I am not a Virginian, but an American."

Besides Patrick Henry, other prominent delegates to this meeting who had already been active in the struggle against parliamentary taxation were George Washington from Virginia, Samuel and John Adams of Massachusetts, John Rutledge of South
Carolina, John Dickinson of Pennsylvania, and Roger Sherman
of Connecticut. Delegates from New England and the South generally wanted to take decisive action. Delegates from the Middle
Colonies were more moderate in their views.

TAKING A FIRM STAND

Differences between the delegates were brought to a head on
September 17 when Paul Revere arrived at Carpenter's Hall with
a series of resolves from Suffolk County, Massachusetts, the
county in which Boston lay. These Suffolk Resolves urged direct
resistance to the Intolerable Acts and stated that Massachusetts'
taxes should be withheld from the crown until the colony's government had been "placed upon a constitutional foundation."

They stated that the jailing of any patriot leader gave the citizens the right to imprison "every servant of the present tyrannical and unconstitutional government" and urged the colony to prepare to resist a British invasion. The Congress applauded the resolves, although the moderate Joseph Galloway of Pennsylvania expressed alarm that they "contained a complete declaration of war against Great Britain." The next day, however, Congress backed off a bit and could only approve the "wisdom and fortitude, with which opposition to these wicked ministerial measures has hitherto been conducted...."

Ten days later, Galloway offered a more moderate approach with his Galloway Plan. It suggested a union of the colonies something like that which the Albany Plan had outlined some twenty years before. It would provide for a separate American legislature called the Grand Council whose members would be elected by the colonial assemblies. This council would have the right to veto all Parliamentary legislation affecting the colonies yet would still be inferior to Parliament, which would have the right to initiate legislation relating to the colonies and which would appoint a President General who would exercise executive authority over the colonies. The main idea behind Galloway's plan was that "no law should bind America without her consent." Nine years before, under the threat of the Stamp Act, some colonial leaders had said that Parliament had the right to pass laws for the colonies but not to tax them. By 1774, however, many were questioning whether Parliament had the right to legislate for them at all. Enough of the delegates to the first Continental Congress agreed and voted down the Galloway Plan by the narrow margin of six colonies to five.

By rejecting Galloway's plan, the delegates were in effect ignoring the instructions they had been given, which were to seek ways to reconcile differences with Britain. On October 8, Congress explicitly approved the Suffolk Resolves. Six days later, it approved its most important document, the Declaration of Rights and Resolves, which a committee had been working on for over a month. Never before had a collection of colonies decided to rebel against the mother country, so the Congress struggled to provide a justification for their acts of rebellion. The Declaration of Rights and Resolves made it clear that the colonies were defying their mother country on the grounds that their rights as Englishmen had been violated. It further insisted on the right of assembly and petition, the right to be free of a standing army, and the right to choose their own councils. It flatly rejected Parliament's right to tax the colonies in any way other than its traditional role of regulating commerce. What the First Continental Congress was really asking was for the British crown to return to the old colonial policy of benign neglect which had existed prior to the French and Indian War and to abandon its new policies of taxing and regulating its American colonies.

On October 20, Congress resolved that every colony should create an "Association," which was a covenant among the people not to import or export goods from or to Great Britain, or to consume any expensive luxuries. Because the boycott of 1770, which had been enforced by the merchants, had not succeeded, association committees would take charge of the task of enforcing the boycott. The Nonimportation and Nonconsumption Agreements were scheduled to go into effect on December 1, 1774. Virginia pleaded for a two-year delay so that she could sell her tobacco crops and seek out new markets. The Congress compromised and granted her a year's delay. South Carolina then demanded that rice and indigo be exempted from the Agreement and promptly walked out of the Congress. The delegates returned only when Congress again compromised by exempting rice from the ban. Nevertheless, some bitterness remained among the delegates.

After these compromises had been all worked out, Congress agreed to meet again in Philadelphia on May 10, 1775, unless all the problems with the mother country had been resolved by then. Charles Thomson aptly summarized the situation in a letter he wrote to Benjamin Franklin, who was in London at the time: "Even yet the wound may be healed and peace and love restored. But we are on the brink of a precipice."

Tensions between England and the colonies were quickly escalating, and the Nonimportation and Nonconsumption Agreements were certain to provoke strong reaction by the British. The delegates of the First Continental Congress knew that Boston had been cut off from the rest of Massachusetts and was now under siege. By January 1775, General Gage would receive authorization from King George III to use force, if necessary, to impose British rule in any of the colonies.

As the delegates returned to their homes, the question of what to do next was on everyone's mind. Diplomatically, the appeals from the colonies to the King were answered only with more British troops. Militarily, the colonies were at a distinct disadvantage. England, on the other hand, had the strongest and best army and navy in the world.

In February, Lord North proposed a set of initiatives that would stop direct taxation of the colonies, but only with the provision that the assemblies had to provide enough money to cover the salaries of British officials. He also refused to recognize the Continental Congress and promised to only deal directly with the colonies. There was little room for agreement, as Parliament had already approved a declaration to the king, stating that the colonies were already in rebellion and should be brought under English sovereignty even if it were against their will.

Few doubted that with this turn of events, what was happening in Boston would spread to all of the colonies if there were any further resistance. Since the appeals to the king were going unanswered, and no real movement towards peace appeared on either side, the choice for the colonists was either submission or heightened resistance.

ORATOR OF FREEDOM

One man who reflected heavily on the situation was Patrick Henry. His fiery oratory was already legendary. He had taken on the established church in the Parson's Cause and he actively continued to defend unlicensed preachers in Virginia. He led the opposition in the House of Burgesses against the Stamp Act a decade earlier and was now one of the leading political figures in America. Before he left for Virginia after the Congress, he met with John Adams for dinner and discussed the situation. Adams read to him a letter from a friend back in Massachusetts, which urged a military plan of action. Adams would later write, "In the Congress of 1774, there was not one member, except Patrick Henry, who appeared to me sensible of the precipice, or rather, the pinnacle on which we stood, and had the candor and courage enough to acknowledge it."

As he traveled back home to Virginia, the question of what to do weighed heavy on Henry. But upon his arrival home, he would be greeted with devastating news—his wife, Sarah, who suffered from an unknown mental illness, was very sick and near death. But the urgent matters of state could not wait. Governor Dunmore refused all requests to reconvene the House of Burgesses, and an effort was underway to call a convention to discuss how the colony would respond to the growing British threat. The Hanover County Committee elected Henry to represent them at the convention on February 18th, but he was absent from the proceedings. Just a week earlier, his wife had died. He told his closest friends how deeply his wife's death grieved him, but he also felt that he couldn't disappoint the people of Virginia in their hour of need.

The Virginia Convention was convened in Richmond on March 20, 1775 at St. John's Church with the leading men of the colony present. The first order of business was a discussion of what had transpired in Philadelphia and to share news of the ongoing siege of Boston from the various committees of correspondence. The news was not encouraging, and many leaders in the other colonies were uncertain how to respond.

Despite his grief and recent personal loss, Patrick Henry put forward a motion for Virginia to take defensive measures against the British threat and prepare plans for calling and arming the militia. The convention was split on the motion. Richard Henry Lee and several of the more militant members supported Henry. Others, such as Peyton Randolph, were cautious that such a move might provoke the British to bring troops to Virginia and impose order. If approved, Henry's motion could mean war. But everyone there knew that by discussing the motion, the convention was flirting with treason. As was the case with the Boston Tea Party, Henry was making a bold move.

Discussion raged back and forth between the convention members. No one, including Henry, was anxious for an armed conflict against the most powerful country in the world. But he concluded that the time for talk and half-measures was over—immediate action was necessary. Failure to do anything would leave Virginia and the whole of America vulnerable to attack by the British.

LIBERTY OR DEATH

Having heard his proposal denounced as going too far, he asked to speak. Rising from the church pew with determination, he knew that the other members of the convention had to be brought to the point where they acknowledged the gravity of the situation. He began his address by acknowledging that despite their differences, all of those present were friends and apologized in advance to those who disagreed with him for the bold statement he was about to make. This was no time for polite conversation: "The question before the House is one of awful moment to this country. For my own part, I consider it as nothing less than a question of freedom or slavery.... Should I keep back my opinions at such a time, through fear of giving offense, I should consider myself as guilty of treason towards my country, and of an act of disloyalty towards the majesty of Heaven, which I revere above all earthly things."

Now that he had everyone's attention and had created in his hearers' minds a sense of anticipation, he wanted to state his case as clearly as possible. Surely, everyone wanted peace, but they had to recognize the threat that the British troops represented. With more and more arriving every day, they were not intended to bring peace, but submission. He continued, "Has Great Britain any enemy in this quarter of the world, to call for all this accumulation of navies and armies? No sir, she has none. They are meant for us: they can be meant for no other. They are sent over to bind and rivet upon us those chains which the British ministry have been so long forging."

Directing his attention to the arguments of those who wanted to make further appeals to the king, he said, "Our petitions have been slighted; our remonstrances have produced additional violence and insult; our supplications have been disregarded; and we have been spurned with contempt from the foot of the throne." The concern was not just with Lord North or the Parliament; this policy of submission extended all the way to the king. Having identified that the problem started at the top and worked its way down to the colonies, there was no room left to hope for yet another appeal to the king: "We must fight! I repeat it sir,—we must fight! An appeal to arms, and to the God of hosts, is all that is left us."

Now that their attention was drawn away from the arguments at hand, he had to address their fears about the British might: "Sir, we are not weak, if we make a proper use of those means which the God of nature hath placed in our power. Three millions of people armed in the holy cause of liberty, and in such a country as that which we possess, are invincible by any force which our enemy can send against us."

Growing all the bolder and speaking now like an Old Testament prophet, he assured them that because their cause was just, their hope should be in the Lord: "There is a God who presides over the destinies of nations, and who will raise up friends to fight our battles for us. The battle sir, is not to the strong alone: it is to the vigilant, the active, the brave." Henry now had to make sure that everyone understood that there was only one course of action to follow: "There is no retreat but in submission and slavery. Our chains are forged. Their clanking may be heard on the plains of Boston. The war is inevitable. And let it come! I repeat it, sir, let it come!"

Summoning what strength he had left in him, he challenged his colleagues to be men of purpose, men of virtue, men of action: "Why stand we here idle? What is it that gentlemen wish? What would they have? Is life so dear, or peace so sweet, as to be purchased at the price of chains and slavery? Forbid it Almighty God!" With his audience sitting motionless and hanging seemingly on every word, Henry wanted those present to have no lingering doubts about where he stood or what was at stake: "I know not what course others may take, but as for me," he said throwing a defiant fist in the air, "give me liberty," and now bringing his hand down to his heart as if holding a dagger, "or give me death!"

Patrick Henry had made his case. The atmosphere in St. John's Church was electric and yet deathly silent. And as he sat down in the pew, one observer later recalled that the words "to arms" quivered on every lip. Another listener was so moved as he stood outside and listened through an open window in the church that he requested to be buried on that spot—a request that was granted at his death. Henry had thrown down the gauntlet, and the members of the convention would pick it up. His motion was approved. Virginia—and America—was now preparing for war.

DIVE DEEPER: PATRICK HENRY

It was on the fourth day of the Second Virginia Convention when Henry (1736-1799) kindled the fires of the American Revolution with blazing words that would forever alter the course of this continent: "Is life so dear, or peace so sweet, as to be purchased at the price of chains and slavery? Forbid it, Almighty God. I know not what course others may take, but as for me, give me liberty or give me death."

As he spoke, he was in the presence of all the greatest luminaries of the day—Washington, Jefferson, Randolph, Harrison, Wythe, Braxton, and Lee—but he would later say that there was only one witness to his oratory that he was actually concerned to please: "It was my foremost occupation to please the Master of the House. For with His approval, I could not help but to accomplish goodly ends."

Because the colonial legislative assembly had been dissolved by order of the royal governor, Lord Dunmore, the leaders of the Burgesses had abandoned Williamsburg, then capital of the Dominion, and had gathered some miles inland, just above the James River shoals on Church Hill in the city of Richmond. A local pastor, Miles Seldon, offered to open his small chapel to the convention—an offer the men gratefully accepted. And so it was that Patrick Henry's famous speech was delivered on March 23, 1775 in the makeshift accommodations of St. John's, the Henrico Parish Church. The "Master of the House" that he so desired to please was, thus, the Lord Himself.

Henry later said, "Of all the honors that have befallen me in this life, the chief is that Providence afforded me the privilege of delivering such an address in such a place. Before the very presence of God Almighty, I made appeal for right. The affairs that followed have indeed vindicated our cause and wed our destiny with the cause of Heaven."

That insight helps to explain how and why Henry devoted himself to public affairs throughout his life. He was, after all, a devout Christian and thus was under no illusions about the relative significance of temporal affairs in the light of eternity. He was a committed family man and thus was keenly aware of the intrusion of public concerns into private duties. And he was a southern agrarian and thus was decidedly diffident about the cosmopolitan diversions of civic involvement.

Like so many of the other revolutionary leaders of his day, the most notable aspect of Patrick Henry's character was that he was not particularly revolutionary. Thus, like those other protagonists in America's epic conflict—from Samuel Adams and John Hancock to James Iredell and Henry Laurens—he was a profoundly conservative man in both manner and resolve. He was loath to indulge in any kind of radicalism that had the potential to erupt into violence—rhetorical, political, or martial. He was a faithful son of the colonial gentry. He was devoted to the time-honored conventions of Whig representative covenant-alism: the rule of law, *noblesse oblige*, unswerving honor, squirely superintendence, and the maintenance of corporate order. He believed in a tranquil and settled society free of the raucous up-sets and tumults of agitation, activism, and unrest. In short, Pat-rick Henry was very much a man of his time and place.

He was second of eleven children—descended from solid Scot-tish Presbyterian stock. He worked hard—as a planter, a shopkeep-er, and a country lawyer. In addition, he was the primary educa-tor of his children—teaching them Greek, Latin, Logic, Rhetoric, History, and Classical Literature. And as if that weren't enough, he kept himself busy in his work as a vestryman at church, as the sponsor of several missions to the frontier, as a some-time delegate to the House of Burgesses, and as an informal rotating instructor at a local Presbyterian Meetinghouse.

He was too busy with the ordinary responsibilities of life to involve himself in radical politics. His Christian faith was too deeply ingrained to dislodge his attentions from what he called "those essential permanent things."

In that regard, he was not alone of course. The reticence of virtually all the notable colonials to squabble with the crown or to dally in political petulance was obvious to even the most casu-al observer. They exhausted all recourse to law before they even thought to resort to armed resistance. For more than a decade, they sent innumerable appeals, suits, and petitions to both par-liament and king. Even after American blood had been spilled, they refrained from impulsive insurrection.

It took more than the Boston Massacre, more than Lexington and Concord, more than Bunker Hill, more than Falmouth, and more than Ticonderoga to provoke the patriots to commit themselves to forceful secession. Even as late as the first week of July 1776, there was no solid consensus among the members of the Continental Congress that "such an extreme as full-scale revolt," as John Dickinson dubbed it, was necessary. That week, the Declaration of Independence drafted by a committee composed of Benjamin Franklin, Roger Sherman, Robert Livingston, John Adams, and the young Thomas Jefferson, was defeated twice before it was diffidently adopted—and even then, the cautious delegates managed to keep its pronouncements secret for four more days. And though Patrick Henry was an early advocate of independence, he did not arrive at that conviction easily or casually.

Like virtually all his fellow patriots he was, at best, a reluctant revolutionary. Why then did he rebel? What could possibly have so overcome his native conservatism? Why would such a naturally taciturn man seek to rouse his comrades to insurrection—however valiant the cause?

It was his abiding Christian worldview, his commitment to those lasting things, both in heaven and on earth, which transcend the ever-shifting tides of situation and circumstance, that finally drove him to action. He resolved to challenge king and motherland in order to preserve all that which king and motherland had always represented before: justice, mercy, and humility before God.

Henry actually abhorred worldly affairs, but he was thrust into the affairs of the world. His ultimate concern was the world into which he would someday go, but he devoted much of his career to the world into which he had already come. He forged a practical balance between the temporal and eternal as the best expression of authentic Christian faithfulness.

Patrick Henry had his priorities straight. His worldview was sound. His passion for justice—which made him an oratorical firebrand—was carefully balanced by an equal passion for mercy and spiritual humility, which made him a statesman rather than just a politician.

CHAPTER 8: PREPARING FOR WAR

"Let us humbly commit our righteous cause to the great Lord of the Universe. Let us joyfully leave our concerns in the hands of Him who raises up and puts down the empires and kingdoms of the earth as He pleases."

JOHN HANCOCK

No sooner had Patrick Henry's words dissolved into the air of St. John's Church that evening than the atmosphere in the colonies profoundly changed. The bluntness of his message and the erosion of any hope for compromise fell heavily upon the listeners, and they responded to his call of urgent action. It was clear to Henry and the other members of the Virginia Convention that the British government was pursuing a policy to push the colonies to the point of unconditional surrender. As Henry said, the choice for the Americans was either submission and slavery or a resort to arms.

The escalation of hostilities by the British did not necessarily receive unanimous support back in England. Two British statesmen and distinguished members of Parliament, William Pitt and Edmund Burke, called on their colleagues to repeal the Intolerable Acts and abandon schemes to tax the colonies.

Unknown to the members of the Virginia Convention, the day before Patrick Henry gave his stirring "Give me Liberty or give me Death" address, Burke delivered an appeal to the House of Commons, later titled "On Conciliation with America," advocating a reversal of British policy and urging his colleagues to make a peaceful settlement with the Americans. Praising their love of liberty, which they had received as part of their English heritage, Burke affirmed the complaint of the colonies that they had no representation in Parliament and yet were required to pay taxes to the Crown.

REBELS, ONE AND ALL

The efforts of Burke and Pitt proved to be fruitless. Parliament refused to receive the Continental Congress's petition and declared that "rebellion existed in the American colonies." On March 30th, King George approved a new act that severely regulated trade between New England and Britain and her possessions. Back in Boston, General Gage marched his Redcoats through the streets of Cambridge and Watertown to demonstrate his intentions to force compliance of the Intolerable and Port Acts.

On both sides of the Atlantic, there was no doubt that these new measures represented a deepening of the conflict. And the colonists responded in kind. England, the mother country, had now unmistakably turned against her willful child, America. But the winds of change did not arrive unexpectedly. This moment, and the times to follow, had been building for years. Since the Seven Years' War and the coronation of King George III, the British had initiated a political revolution by extending the reach of the government into colonial affairs and claiming absolute authority over the lives of its subjects—a controversy most thought had been resolved by the English Civil War and the Glorious Revolution over a hundred years before.

WHERE THE SPIRIT OF THE LORD IS

Meanwhile, a new Reformation, born of the spiritual changes wrought by the Great Awakening, had taken firm root in America. As William McLoughlin, a modern historian attests, "the roots of the Revolution as a political movement were so deeply imbedded in the soil of the First Great Awakening forty years earlier that it can be truly said that the Revolution was the natural outgrowth of that profound and widespread religious movement."

No less an authority than John Adams testified to the pervasive effects of the Great Awakening on the American conscience in the days and years leading up to the War for Independence: "The Revolution was effected before the war commenced. The Revolution was in the minds and hearts of the people; a change in their religious sentiments of their duties and obligations. This radical change in the principles, opinions, sentiments and affections of the people was the real American revolution."

But what were these changes in the religious beliefs and practices of the colonists that were reflected in their response to the looming British threat? The first was the institutional break between church and state. Many of the settlers of New England were religious refugees fleeing persecution from the Anglican Church. In the Mid-Atlantic and Southern states, dissenting Presbyterians and Baptists still struggled with the Anglican establishment over issues of freedom of conscience and preaching without government licenses. Because the Great Awakening had been started by itinerants and sustained by ministers who rejected any association with the Anglican Church, many of the citizens in the hot spots of the Revolution had no attachments to the established religion of England.

Another major factor was the shift in expectations regarding the Second Coming of Christ. While the dominant belief in the Old World was that the progress of history was going to devolve until the rise of the Antichrist, when Christ would return to rescue his Church and put an end to history, the Puritans who arrived in New England believed that they were on a divine mission to build the Kingdom of God and usher in a thousand-year era of peace and prosperity where the Gospel would flourish under the Reign of Christ.

The Great Awakening revived these old Puritan beliefs. In 1742, Jonathan Edwards published his work, *Thoughts on the Revival in New England*, in which he expressed his hopes that the religious work in America would be the beginning of a glorious Christian age: "We cannot reasonably think otherwise than that the beginning of this great work of God must be near," Edwards said. "And there are many things that make it probable that this work will begin in America." During the Seven Years' War with France, pastors warned their congregations about the horrors that would unfold in America if the Roman Catholic forces were to prevail. But they believed then that God was on the side of the

British and that they would be victorious. Samuel Davies, the Presbyterian pastor to Patrick Henry and later president of the College of New Jersey, in a sermon entitled "Serious Reflections on War," delivered in 1757, hailed the events of the Seven Years' War as that time when "the Kingdom of Christ, the Prince of Peace, shall be extended over the world, and his benign, pacific religion shall be propagated among all nations."

But as the relations between England and America worsened over the next decade, the pastors adapted their message to the new situation. Rather than battling the forces of Roman Catholicism, the Antichrist was now the forces of tyranny and absolutism that were taking hold back in the mother country. By opposing the political tyranny of Parliament and King George and the spiritual tyranny and corruption of the established church in England, the colonists were preparing the way for the Millennium of Christ. This was the religious climate resulting from the Great Awakening that birthed and justified the colonial resistance.

THUNDERING PULPITS

Throughout the colonies, other religious movements were underway that would support the growing movement of dissent. In New England, ministers regularly delivered sermons on various occasions that addressed the political affairs of the day. The most common type was the Election Day sermon, which was preached every year in the presence of the governor and the newly elected members of the legislature to remind them of their duties as civil magistrates and the requirement that they act both virtuously and justly in their public office. These sermons were printed and widely distributed amongst the colonies and had been delivered in Massachusetts and Connecticut since the founding of the colonies. The sermons preached on Election Day were accompanied by several other types of sermons for other events: the Artillery Sermon, which was preached when new militia officers were selected; the Thanksgiving Day Sermon, which was delivered on special occasions to mark a particular demonstration of God's providence in national or international affairs—such as the repeal of the Stamp Act; the Fast Day Sermon, which was preached in times of calamity and was accompanied by public calls for repentance; and sermons preached annually to commemorate the execution of Charles I in 1649 and the Glorious Revolution of 1688.

In the years leading up to the War for Independence, the Election Day sermons were the primary vehicle used by the pastors in New England to articulate their political ideals and justify resistance to British oppression. The most famous of these, *A Discourse concerning Unlimited Submission and Non-Resistance to the Higher Powers*, was delivered by the Boston pastor Jonathan Mayhew on the anniversary of the execution of Charles I by the Puritan Parliament for treason. This address laid out the common themes of the Election Day sermons: rulers were to govern for the benefit of all the people, not to themselves; officials were bound by the same laws as other citizens and by the requirement to obey God's laws in the administration of justice; subjects had a right to appeal to lower magistrates to restrain unlawful activity by government officers and had the undeniable right to take up arms when life and liberty were threatened.

In the tumultuous days of 1775, Samuel Langdon, president of Harvard College, delivered a sermon that chastised the British government for trying to force the colonists to submit to their tyrannical rule: "Our King," Langdon said, "as if impelled by some strange fatality, is resolved to reason with us only by the roar of his cannon, and the printed arguments of muskets and bayonets. Because we refuse submission to the despotic power of a ministerial Parliament, our own sovereign [...] has given us up to the rage of his ministers."

The effect of these sermons did not go unnoticed by the British authorities. In 1774, the Governor of Massachusetts denied a request by the colonial assembly to convene a fast day, because he said it would only afford an opportunity for "sedition to flow from the pulpits."

But the religious motive for taking up arms was not limited to New England. In Pennsylvania, Virginia, and the Carolinas, both the Presbyterians and the Baptists were taking up the cause of freedom. Angered by the Quebec Act, which gave the Roman Catholics in Canada the religious freedoms that they were denied in their own colonies, the dissenting clergy had been active since the Great Awakening in developing political principles that were now being used to persuade the colonies to prepare for war.

It isn't hard to understand how these pastors became as influential as they did. In New England, the Congregationalist clergy were from the most well-respected families in the area. The Presbyterian ministers further south were generally the most educated men in their communities. The prominent Lutheran pastor of Pennsylvania, Henry Muhlenburg, wrote in his journal about the reasons for the Presbyterians success: "This progress is due to the fact that they have established seminaries in various places, educate their own ministers, keep strict discipline, and tolerate no ministers except those who have good moral character and the ability to speak, and who are content with small salaries and able to endure hard work. Those denominations here which do not have these characteristics, but just the opposite, are consequently decreasing and making room for the Presbyterians."

The massive waves of Scotch-Irish immigration up until 1775 flooded all of the colonies with adherents of the Presbyterian faith. Representing one of the largest people groups in America, they had built numerous communities in virtually every colony and developed extensive networks to keep in contact with one another, but their presence was particularly felt in Virginia. Here Presbyterian churches sprung up like wildflowers, with fiery pastors, many of whom fled from their homeland because of religious and political persecution by the English. It was in one of these churches that the young Patrick Henry would listen to the fervent sermons of Samuel Davies and learn to develop his own passionate rhetorical style.

By the time Davies left Virginia, there were many younger Presbyterian pastors to take his place. Having graduated from the Log College and the College of New Jersey, these men were instructed not only in religious studies, but also in civil matters. There they learned about the natural law established by God that governed the universe and the affairs of men and the political theories of the leaders of the Reformation. Traveling up and down the backwoods of Virginia, Maryland, Pennsylvania, the Carolinas, and Georgia, these itinerants preached against the Parliamentary claims of absolute power and about the rights of citizens to punish government officials that violated both the written law and the law of God. Reminded of their Scottish

Covenanter ancestors that had paid with their lives in defense of their liberties, Presbyterian ministers, like Alexander Craighead, John and Samuel Blair, Samuel Finley, John Rodgers, and Alexander McWhorter, encouraged their congregations to take up arms for the sake of their freedoms that were under attack once again by the British government.

As hostilities increased and preparations were being made for war, the Baptists became important allies for the leaders of the resistance. It was no wonder, for up until 1775, the Baptists were actively persecuted in the colonies. Patrick Henry had to defend many of their ministers against Virginia authorities. Their services were frequently disrupted by angry mobs and their clergy were regularly horsewhipped or had their tongues nailed to posts for preaching without government licenses. They rejected the dancing, drinking, and gambling commonplace in gentry society, and they believed in the equality of all their members. Their entire lifestyle was a rejection of British culture.

Their growth was explosive. In 1769, there were just seven Baptists churches in Virginia. By 1775, there were fifty-four. As the opening shots of the War for Independence were fired, the Baptist leader, Isaac Backus, would appeal to his congregation to take up arms to defend their freedoms, noting that nothing less than their fundamental freedom to worship as their consciences dictated was at stake.

By April 1775, the clergy of America were not only solidly behind the defensive efforts of the colonial leaders, but they were also leading the charge against British oppression. In their sermons, they called for their congregations to take action, encouraging them to "obey God rather than men." Many pastors would leave their pulpits to take up arms themselves and lead the men of their congregations into battle. In the opening days of the conflict, the motto "disobedience to tyrants is obedience to God" seemed to be uttered by every American speaker and writer, without the slightest hint of embarrassment that colonial religion was shaping their politics. Everyone, of any religious belief, knew that faith in the Judge of all Nations was necessary now that the colonies were poised on a dark and deadly threshold with nothing less than their lives and liberties on the line.

GUN CONTROL:
OVER OUR DEAD BODIES

Indeed, before May 1775 came around, events were about to take place that would push the colonies over that threshold. The Massachusetts Government Act had removed Governor Hutchinson and replaced him with General Gage in the summer of 1774. Gage's effort to keep that colony's legislature from meeting was to no avail. Meeting first at Salem, and later at Cambridge and Concord, they set up a Committee of Safety that began to collect and store gunpowder and other military supplies to defend themselves against the British. Outside the city of Boston, this Committee of Safety became the actual colonial government.

On the night of April 18, 1775, General Gage sent troops to seize the guns and ammunition, which the Committee of Safety had stored some twenty miles inland from Boston in Concord, Massachusetts. He also planned to arrest Samuel Adams and John Hancock, two leaders of the Sons of Liberty who were staying in Lexington, six miles east of Concord. Gage had tried to keep this move a secret, but somehow, the word got out about two hours before the troops marched from their barracks that night. Paul Revere and William Dawes, active Sons of Liberty, waited for word from a third man who was stationed in the steeple of Christ Church, Boston, (nicknamed the Old North Church) to see whether the British soldiers would march by land across the narrow neck which led to their barracks or whether they would row across the harbor to Charlestown to begin their march. The prearranged signal would be "One if by land and two if by sea." When a first and then a second lantern was lit, Revere and Dawes knew that the soldiers would row to Charlestown to begin their march.

Riding together well ahead of the British forces, Revere and Dawes alerted the Massachusetts militia, the Minutemen. They called themselves Minutemen because they claimed that they could be ready to march at a minute's notice. Late that night, Revere was captured and questioned by a British patrol and then released. He soon rejoined Dawes. The two of them continued to alert the Minutemen as they made their way toward Lexington. Between Lexington and Concord, Revere and Dawes met Dr. Samuel Prescott, a Lexington physician who had been to Concord to visit his fiancée. He joined in the effort to make sure that as many militiamen as possible were ready to face the British Redcoats when they arrived.

THE SHOT HEARD ROUND THE WORLD

When the main British force of about seven hundred arrived in Lexington early on the morning of April 19, they were faced by just seventy Minutemen. As the British commander was ordering them to disperse, an unknown person fired a musket.

Both sides took that as a signal to start firing. When they had finished, eight Minutemen were killed and ten were wounded. One Redcoat was slightly wounded and the British delayed by about fifteen minutes.

The British continued on to Concord, about six miles down the road, which they entered without resistance around eight o'clock. There they destroyed some supplies and a few gun carriages, although most of the gunpowder had already been moved to another location. Meanwhile, some three or four hundred minutemen returned and tried to take the North Bridge. The British fired first. In a famous poem by Ralph Waldo Emerson:

> Here once embattled farmers stood,
> And fired the shot heard round the world.

The gun battle lasted only five minutes. Two Americans and three British soldiers lay dead. Nine more British were wounded, but the battle was far from over.

BLOODY RETREAT

The British retreat to Boston was a foretaste of the fighting which would baffle and frustrate the British for the rest of this conflict. On the way to Lexington, Minutemen fired from barns and farmhouses and from behind stone walls, fences, and trees. In all, some three to four thousand Minutemen rained lead upon the hapless Redcoats. By the time Lexington came into view, the British had broken into a run. In mid-afternoon, a relief force of twelve hundred men from Boston came to their rescue.

The bloody retreat to Boston cost the British seventy killed, one hundred sixty-five wounded, and twenty-six missing, in addition to the thirteen earlier casualties. In all, the British lost over two hundred seventy men while the Americans lost ninety-five. British soldiers who had once sneered at the fighting ability of the Americans now had a different opinion.

Jonas Clark, the pastor of the church in Lexington and the host for Sam Adams and John Hancock on the night that the troops arrived, surveyed the scene on Lexington Green the following day. Recognizing that many of the men killed were from his congregation and realizing the tragedy that had just struck the families of his community, he was still able to comprehend the enormity of the event. Walking amongst the fallen men, he told an observer, "From this day will be dated the liberty of the world." Reports of the battle swept through the colonies. Everywhere, people began to prepare for a pitched battle for freedom. The time for compromise had ended. The War for American Independence had begun.

CHAPTER 9: WARS AND RUMORS OF WARS

"Of all the tyrannies, a tyranny sincerely expressed for the good of its victims may be the most oppressive. It may be better to live under robber barons than under omnipotent busybodies."

C.S. LEWIS

On the morning of April 19, 1775, American and British bodies littered the town squares of Concord and Lexington and the roads leading from there to Boston. The first engagement of the American War of Independence had been fought with significant losses to both sides but with a clear moral victory for the Americans. The communication networks established by the Committee of Safety were successful in not only warning Sam Adams and John Hancock of the approaching British forces but also in raising the alarm to bring enough minutemen from the surrounding countryside to fight off the British squadrons and send them fleeing back to Boston.

One young associate of Sam Adams, Dr. Joseph Warren, had been in the middle of the fray. Even as shots were flying by him, he tended to the wounded on the battlefield and was instantly proclaimed a hero. But with the members of the Committee for Safety taking refuge outside the reach of the British military, Warren now found himself in charge of operations. In the name of the Committee for Safety, he drafted a report on April 28th giving a description of the battle to be sent by messengers to the outlying towns of Massachusetts, Connecticut, and Providence Plantations. It concluded with an urgent appeal for men at arms: "Our all is at stake. Death and devastation are the instant consequence of delay. Every moment is infinitely precious. An hour lost may deluge your country in blood and entail perpetual slavery upon the few of your posterity who may survive the carnage."

But even before the message was sent, armed men hungry for battle were moving towards Boston. A militia lieutenant in Connecticut, Israel Putnam, received the report of the battles, left his plow, and rode for eighteen hours without stopping to join up with the colonial forces. A contingent of men arrived from New Hampshire after marching fifty-five miles in less than a day. Benedict Arnold, the commander of the New Haven, Connecticut militia, argued with the town selectmen about his request for munitions for him and his men and left for Massachusetts only after threatening to break into the powder house and take what they needed. Hundreds and thousands of men arrived after hearing the news of the battle. In just a few days, more than 20,000 men were present and ready to fight.

Joseph Warren set up headquarters in Harvard Yard in Cambridge and began to organize the forces into an army to encircle

Boston. Knowing that he had General Gage and the British army trapped in the city, Warren called for eight thousand men to enlist for up to seven months to lay siege to Gage's troops. On April 23, the Massachusetts Provincial Congress, which was already in session at the time of the battle, called for a force of 30,000 troops, with 13,500 coming from their own colony. Connecticut followed suit and raised 6,000 of its own men. New Hampshire pledged 2,000 men, and Rhode Island promised three regiments. As far south as Charleston, South Carolina, the Provincial Congress raised three regiments and appropriated £140,000 for the new colonial army.

In addition, the Massachusetts Congress drafted an account of the battle of Lexington to send to England. It noted that the British troops opened fire first and that the battle was purely defensive, and it offered a list of their grievances against the government's policy. They made it clear that the events had "not yet detached us from our royal sovereign; we profess to be his loyal and dutiful subjects, and though hardly dealt with, as we have been, are still ready with our lives and fortunes, to defend his person, crown, and dignity." But they were hardly apologetic, for the appeal continued: "Nevertheless, to the persecution and tyranny of his evil ministry, we will not tamely submit. Appealing to heaven for the justice of our cause, we determine to die or be free." The colonists were not yet ready to sever their ties with England, but the line was drawn. They refused to submit to British oppression.

ADVANTAGE: FREEDOM

Back in England, the members of Parliament and the King's Cabinet were certain of a quick victory. They sneered at the "backwoods" colonials who had neither the talent nor the resources to take on the greatest military power in the world and conduct a lengthy war. The British were confident in their abilities, but in America, the colonials were now being driven by a desperate need to preserve their freedom. What they lacked in material supplies or training, they would make up in spirit and determination.

It was this love of liberty that, in a matter of a few hours, shifted the military advantage from the British troops, hunting for Adams and Hancock, to the Americans, who now had the British trapped in Boston. All of the colonies rallied to the cause of their fellow colonists in Massachusetts, and the news of the recent events inflamed the whole of America. One Lutheran pastor in Philadelphia described the effect that the battles at Lexington and Concord had on the colonial spirit: "Throughout the whole country great preparations are making for the war, and almost every person is under arms [...]. Neighborhoods, concerning which it would have been expected that years would be required to induce them voluntarily to take up arms, became strongly inclined for war as soon as the battle of Lexington was known. Quakers and Mennonites take part in the military exercises, and in great numbers renounce their former religious principles. The hoarse din of war is hourly heard in our streets."

The prompt formation of the colonial militias into a colonial army was not accidental. The British were now paying the price of their own policy—in the Seven Years' War, they had encouraged the creation of colonial militias to face the French and

Indian threat. Massachusetts Governor Thomas Pownall encouraged local militias during that conflict by reminding the citizens "a free government depends on no other soldiery but its own citizens for its defense [...] so every freeholder should be a soldier." But now that the American enemy was no longer France, but British tyranny, the very instrument that they created was now being used against them.

PEACE THROUGH STRENGTH

For the colonies, the militias reflected ideological commitments as well as practical military concerns. As part of their own British legacy, they had learned the lessons of history and realized the value of maintaining armed forces apart from the authority of the King. After the Restoration of Charles II in 1660, he used his appointment power of the militia commanders to bring those forces under his control, which resulted in a significant shift of power from local authorities to the Crown. The colonists also saw how the creation of standing armies under direct authority of the king made the citizens totally dependent on the government for their protection.

But they also looked to ancient history to see how the Israelites, Athenians, Spartans, and Romans used their citizen armies as protection from external threats and internal power struggles. The shift from citizen-soldiers to professional armies led to the demise of all of those former powers, with the Hebrew Republic as the only exception. Both English and colonial writers emphasized the duty of citizens to bear arms for their freedoms whenever a threat arose. By placing the protection of the people in the hands of the citizens, it was hoped that the militias would become schools of virtue rather than troughs of vice. They reasoned that if citizens were reluctant to take up arms, then the country was already corrupted and ripe for any conqueror.

THE PAMPHLETEERS

In the years leading up to the War for Independence, American presses produced a series of tracts and pamphlets emphasizing the duty of the colonies to maintain their own militias. When New York grappled with General Gage over the Townshend Duties, John Trenchard published a series of newspaper articles, entitled *An Argument Shewing that A Standing Army is Inconsistent with a Free Government*, against the use of British troops to enforce the law. In Massachusetts, the leaders of the colony expressed the same concern. In 1774, John Hancock spoke of the need for citizens-soldiers on the commemoration of the Boston Massacre by arguing, "From a well regulated militia we have nothing to fear because their interest is the same with that of the state."

After the Boston Tea Party and the passage of the Port Act, Josiah Quincy, Jr. authored the *Observations on the Boston Port Bill; With Thoughts on Civil Society and Standing Armies*, in which he contrasted the colonial militia, composed of "freeholders, citizen and husbandmen, who take up arms to preserve their property and individuals, and their rights as freemen," with the British Redcoats, who defended the "ambition and power" of corrupt royal agents. John Adams, writing anonymously as *Novanglus*, saw that colonial control of the militia removed the royal grip by replacing "men who procured their commissions from a governor as reward for making themselves pimps to his tools," with local men who were defending their own homes and property beside their neighbors.

The colonies responded to these arguments. In Massachusetts, the Provincial Congress reorganized the colonial militia and placed it under its control of officers elected by and from the people in accordance with the Suffolk Resolves. By the end of 1775, the colonial governments of Maryland, New York, Pennsylvania, Virginia, New Hampshire, and North Carolina had all taken measures to follow Massachusetts' example. The mobilization of the colonial militias after Lexington and Concord was the result of careful thinking and preparation by the colonial assemblies.

Now that conflict had come to the colonies, leadership of the militias was going to be an important key in coordinating strategy and maintaining the discipline of the Continental Army. Bravery and aggressiveness were not in short supply, as witnessed by the urgency of Benedict Arnold to get to Boston and the eagerness of a New Hampshire militia leader, Ethan Allen, to confront the British.

PRESBYTERIAN WARRIORS

More than bravado, the colonies needed experienced military leaders. Fortunately, there were such men available. Arthur St. Clair of Pennsylvania, one of the many experienced military men transplanted from Scotland, was responsible for organizing the militias in his own colony as well as in New Jersey and Delaware. His family was forced out of their ancestral Highland homeland after the defeat of the Jacobite forces of Bonnie Prince Charlie at the Battle of Culloden in 1746. He, however, enrolled in the British army to learn the military arts and strategy of his enemy.

Coming to America while serving as a Redcoat in the Seven Years' War, he chose to stay after the war and settle in one of the Pennsylvania communities established by Scottish immigrants. Detesting the English, he was delighted to be able to assist the colonial militias in establishing an effective defense against his hated British foes. The Second Continental Congress, which reconvened in Philadelphia during May 1775, would look to another Seven Years' War veteran, the Virginian George Washington, to help lead the spirited, but ragtag Continental Army in the early days of the war.

A NEW KIND OF WAR

As the battles of Lexington and Concord demonstrated, this would be a new kind of warfare. The professional army of Redcoats would face the citizen-soldiers of the colonial militia. In terms of weaponry, the British would have a seeming advantage. The infantry carried the "Brown Bess" musket, which was not very accurate, but the large shot it used would cause serious injury anywhere it hit. The colonials had to use whatever weapons were available, but most of the men in the militia were skilled marksmen, as they had to use them for hunting and defense on the frontier.

The British army had large contingents of cavalry and artillery, which would be useful in the close-quarters, mass-formation style of fighting that the English generals preferred. Moving their forces into close range of the enemy, they would fire their initial rounds and then charge with their heavy seventeen-inch bayonets, usually overrunning the colonial forces, who would not have bayonets until later in the war. But once removed from the open field, the Redcoats were susceptible to deadly sniping attacks, similar to what they experienced on their return to Boston after Lexington and Concord. The British could also rely on their navy—the best in the world. But there were many American sailors that had served on British ships, who, under men such as John Paul Jones, would boldly challenge the English fleet all over the open seas.

EVERYTHING TO LOSE

One final difference that played a critical role in the outcome of the War of Independence was that, despite the lack of their training, the Americans had everything to lose and their freedom to gain. This psychological factor gave the Continental Army an edge as they confronted the British regulars. It would also work negatively against the British, as word of atrocities, such as the indiscriminate burning of towns and killing of innocent civilians, served to inflame the colonists and embolden them despite any recent military losses. As Patrick Henry had pointed out, this battle was nothing less than a desperate struggle that meant freedom or slavery for America.

EARLY VICTORIES

An understanding that their liberty was being weighed in the balance is what drove so many men to Boston in the days and weeks after Lexington and Concord. The ranks of this accidental army swelled at the prospect of being able to drive General Gates and his troops out of America. The Americans were eager for action, and they would soon have it.

Indeed, just days after Lexington and Concord, Ethan Allen and his Green Mountain Boys, from the independent Hampshire Grants of Vermont, briefly joined forces with American troops and marched against Fort Ticonderoga on Lake Champlain. The American commander, Benedict Arnold, had urged the Massachusetts Committee of Safety to send a contingent of men to the fort, which was undermanned and dilapidated, to seize the weapons and supplies that were there. The Committee approved a regiment of 400 men. Meanwhile, Samuel Parsons, the commander of a small force from Connecticut, had joined forces with Ethan Allen's Vermont troops to create a small band of 200 irregular militiamen. All three converged two miles from the fort.

They took the British forces at Fort Ticonderoga by surprise on May 10, 1775, the same day that the Second Continental Congress had its opening session, with Allen ordering their surrender "in the name of the great Jehovah and the Continental Congress." This victory netted them ten tons of musket balls, thirty gun carriages, ten cases of gunpowder, and almost 100 cannon.

Two days later, Allen and his Vermont militia quickly took another British position at nearby Crown Point, which gave them control of the entire Champlain Valley. Unfortunately, it also gave the Continental Congress a serious problem. Congress had been planning to tell the world that the Americans were fighting a *defensive* action against British moves, but the capture of these forts was clearly *offensive*. The uncontrolled behavior of the American allies from independent Vermont—Allen's Green Mountain Boys—only gave the British ammunition to paint the Americans as a savage mob.

At the beginning of the congressional session, Peyton Randolph of Virginia was elected again as president of the Congress, but he was soon called away to Virginia to assist in the military preparations taking place there. John Hancock was subsequently elected president. He presided over a complete assembly, as Georgia had been prompted by the events in Massachusetts to send delegates to the gathering.

The first issue raised was whether the troops surrounding Boston should remain under the control of the Massachusetts Provincial Congress or should be placed under the command of the Continental Congress. While debating the issue with the Massachusetts leaders, the Continental Congress unanimously appointed George Washington, after a motion by John Adams, to lead any troops that the Congress might raise. Washington had shown his desire to fight by wearing his colonel's uniform to the congressional meetings. The Congress also sent an appeal to the colonists in Canada in an attempt to enlist their support in the struggle against the British, assuring them that no hostile actions would be taken against them.

THE BATTLE OF BUNKER HILL

While the Continental Congress was considering these issues, the situation in Boston was heating up. Three additional English generals—William Howe, John Burgoyne, and Henry Clinton, all revered veterans of the Seven Years' War—had arrived in late May to join General Gage. Needless to say, the British commanders did not think highly of the gathered colonials. Upon his arrival, Burgoyne was heard to say, "What! Ten thousand peasants keep five thousand king's troops shut up? Well, let us get in, and we'll soon find elbow room." But they would find it easier said than done.

Once hostilities had begun, General Gage had hoped to take the high ground of Bunker Hill and Breed's Hill on the Charlestown peninsula in order to control Boston. But concerned that the British might take the high ground, the Committee of Safety authorized American Colonel William Prescott to seize both hills. His troops, numbering about 1,200, worked all night on June 16, 1775, building an earthen fort on Breed's Hill. Prescott posted sentries to make sure that the sound of the shovels did not raise the attention of the British troops.

When the sun came up and the American position was revealed, the British warships began firing on the troops on Breed's Hill. Confident that his soldiers could storm the hill and drive off the rebels, General Gage ordered an infantry assault under General Howe and also ordered that Charlestown below be set afire to prevent snipers from firing on the massing British troops. As the first rank of fusiliers marched toward the American positions, one of the American commanders, Israel Putnam, encouraged his men to use their ammunition sparingly, saying, "Don't fire until you see the whites of their eyes." As the first rank advanced within yards of the Americans, the order was given to open fire. A blistering rain of bullets fell upon the Redcoats, killing ninety-six of them. The infantrymen right behind climbed over the bodies and were met with the same murderous musket fire. With the officers ordering the British troops to keep advancing, a third charge was made, with deadly consequences. British blood was now running down the hill, turning the water of Boston Harbor red.

General Howe withdrew the men and planned an all-out assault on the American position from three sides of the hill. As the troops moved forward, the Americans made sure to target the officers, killing them with lethal accuracy. In the face of withering American fire, the British soldiers began a hurried retreat back to safety. Now that General Clinton had brought his troops up to the front, Howe planned one last assault. Unknown to him, Colonel Prescott's men at the top of the hill were almost out of ammunition. Some were firing nails and small rocks from their muskets. The Americans fired all they had, killing even more British soldiers, and scrambled up the hill to safety.

The British took control of the entrenched positions, but at a fatal price: 226 dead and 828 wounded, forty-eight percent of Howe's attack forces. More than nineteen officers were killed—more than were killed in the Battle of Quebec in 1759 when England gained control of the whole of Canada—and another seventy officers were wounded. The British generals paid a high price for possession of these small fortifications. The casualties for the colonials included 140 dead and 270 wounded. Among the American dead was Joseph Warren, the hero of Lexington, who had just been commissioned as general.

While the British had driven off the colonials, it had come at a terrible cost. While the Battles of Bunker Hill and Breed's Hill were technically American defeats—they had been forced to retreat—they cost the British heavily and proved that amateur American soldiers could stand and fight the best professional soldiers that England could field.

Just a few months into the conflict, the colonists had won several small engagements and achieved a few moral victories.

But the members of the Continental Congress, still meeting in Philadelphia, knew that a long, costly battle still lay ahead. The Continental Army needed more than moral victories. Retaking Boston was strategic, but it did not remove the massive British military threat. Having met for almost a year, there was still no consensus about what course of action the colonies should take. Efforts were still being made to seek reconciliation with King George. Well into 1776, the Continental Congress was still not seriously considering talk of declaring independence.

"When the news of Lexington and Bunker Hill arrived, parson after parson left his parish and marched hastily toward Boston. Before daylight on the morning of April 30, 1775, Stephen Farrar, of New Ipswich, New Hampshire, left with ninety-seven of his parishioners. Joseph Willard, of Beverly, marched with two companies from his own town, raised in no small part through his own exertion. David Avery, of Windsor, Vermont, after hearing the news of Lexington, preached a farewell sermon, then, outside the meeting-house door, called his people to arms, and marched with twenty men. On his way, he served as captain, preached, and collected more troops. David Grosvenor, of Grafton, left his pulpit and, musket in hand, joined the minute-men who marched to Cambridge. Phillips Payson, of Chelsea, was given credit for leading a group of his parishioners to attack a band of English soldiers that nineteenth day of April. Benjamin Balch, of Danvers, Lieutenant of the third-alarm list of his town, was present at Lexington and later, as chaplain in army and navy, won the title of 'fighting parson.' Jonathan French, of Andover, Massachusetts, left his pulpit on the Sabbath morning, when the news of Bunker Hill arrived, and with surgical case in one hand and musket in the other started for Boston." –Alice Baldwin, *New England Clergy and the American Revolution*

CHAPTER 10: PUSH FOR INDEPENDENCE

"We have staked the whole future of American civilization, not upon the power of government, far from it. We have staked the future upon the capacity of each and all of us to govern ourselves, to sustain ourselves, according to the Ten Commandments of God."

JAMES MADISON

The moral victory achieved on Breed's Hill and Bunker Hill gave the Continental Congress a small measure of confidence, but there were still many undecided issues confronting the assembly. Word of the victories of American commander Benedict Arnold and Vermont commander Ethan Allen at Fort Ticonderoga and Crown Point, just days after the convention opened in May 1775, were well-received. But the pressing problem of how to organize and supply a Continental Army was complicated by the larger problem of how the colonies were to be associated and what actual powers the Congress was to have apart from the direction of the individual colonies. How would this new association be organized, and on what basis would they continue to resist the British Empire?

In retrospect, it is easy to see that the men gathered in Philadelphia were up to the task to answer these questions. They represented the new type of man that only America could build: religious and tolerant; loyal, yet independent; cautious, but determined; deeply principled, and also pragmatic. It was the finest group of men from the colonies that had ever been assembled. The names of those men today are a roster of the heroes of liberty: Sam Adams, John Adams, and John Hancock from Massachusetts; Ben Franklin and Roger Morris of Pennsylvania; Roger Sherman and Oliver Wolcott of Connecticut; George Washington and Richard Henry Lee of Virginia; and Charles Carroll of Maryland, a devout Roman Catholic whose wealth rivaled Hancock's. The Virginia delegation would soon receive a new member—Thomas Jefferson, who arrived to replace Edmund Randolph. These were men already known for their leadership in the colonies, most of them having been involved in the struggle for liberty since the Stamp Act crisis a decade earlier. America needed men such as these to navigate the colonies through the turbulent waters of the struggling resistance to tyranny and to chart a course towards a future of freedom.

LIBERTY AND VIRTUE

While the leaders of the Continental Congress were far from moral perfection, they carried out their offices in a dignified manner and conducted themselves accordingly. Their characters stood in marked contrast to the government officials who devised the British colonial policies for America. The two men who administered the land and sea wars for King George, George Sackville, the Secretary of State for the American colonies, and John Montagu, Earl of Sandwich and First Lord of the Admiralty, were two of the most perverse personalities of the London social scene. Sackville was a known homosexual and maintained an open relationship with a male "domestic partner." One contemporary described Sandwich as "mischievous as a monkey and as lecherous as a goat." Both were highly unpopular and savaged by the British press, which was not generally known for its prudish outlook. One attack was launched against Sackville in 1776 after he appointed two fellow homosexuals, Richard Cumberland and Benjamin Thompson, to high-ranking government positions without any apparent qualification other than their sexual associations. As the British conducted the war against America, the depravity and debauchery of its government ministers and officers in the military high command would harm morale amongst the troops and regularly compromise the military mission they were conducting. As the Americans stiffened in their resolve to fight rather than submit to British oppression, the reputation of the British officials only inflamed colonial resentment and gave them additional reasons to distance themselves from the British Empire.

AMERICANS DEFINED

Patrick Henry had said during the First Continental Congress, "I am an American," but exactly what that meant was still under discussion. There was no consensus as to what political arrangements would be made in each respective colony or in the colonies taken together as a whole. The British governors had disbanded many of the colonial assemblies. The Committees of Safety now ruled several colonies, while others had no governmental structure at all. The colonies would need to begin to organize themselves as separate states with their own systems of government. This would require these new states to adopt their own constitutions. As a result, several members of Continental Congress, including Patrick Henry, returned to their homes to begin forming these state governments.

Furthermore, there were twenty-one British colonies in the Americas, but to date, only thirteen had sent delegations to the Congress—Georgia, which was absent from the First Congress, had just sent representatives for the Second Congress. There were active attempts to bring the Canadian provinces—and even the West Indies plantations—into the fold, but without all of the colonies represented, there were some lingering doubts about whether the Congress was truly representative. To address the need for some structure to link all of the colonies together and for the Congress to govern, Ben Franklin drafted a set of Articles of Federation and Perpetual Union to initiate some discussion of what a national government might look like. The other members were initially cool to Franklin's proposal, and the debate would continue for many months as events continued to unfold and intensify. Some type of federation or confederation was needed to manage the colonies during the course of the war.

HOMELAND SECURITY

Another question arose: What was needed to defend the colonies against the British, and how would the Congress pay for it? Congress first addressed this problem by authorizing the printing of currency worth three million Spanish dollars, with each state being responsible to pay back their share of that amount according to their population and representation in the Congress.

To counter the threat of attack from the North, the Congress authorized Philip Schuyler, Richard Montgomery, and Benedict Arnold to lead their respective forces north to conquer Canada. It would take months to make the necessary preparations to make the trek through the wilderness and launch an effective attack on St. Johns, Quebec, and Montreal. Having secured agreements from the Canadians and the Indian tribes in the region that they would not attack the American forces, they hoped that a victory in Canada would enlist the Canadians in the colonial cause and apply greater pressure on General Gage's troops to force them off the continent.

The members of Congress had also unanimously appointed George Washington as Commander-in-Chief of the Continental Army. When word of the conflict in Boston reached Washington in Philadelphia, he promptly gathered his general staff and aides-de-camp and set off to assume command of the troops around Boston. There were other hopefuls who wanted Washington's position, including Major General Charles Lee who had previously served in the British Army, but they were cautious to wait for their opportunity to demonstrate that the Congress had made the wrong choice.

When Washington arrived to take command, he was troubled by what confronted him. Rather than an organized army responding to his direction, it was a ragtag collection of volunteers who received their orders from the leaders back in the colonies. While the soldiers were skilled marksmen, they had virtually no training in military maneuvers. He also had to deal with many ambitious militia commanders who were eager for prominence and prestige, but not always willing to confront the enemy.

Additionally, Washington discovered that, while he should have had more than 16,000 men under his command, less than 14,000 men were actually present for duty. Although they already outnumbered the British troops in Boston, he still felt that more men would be necessary to man all the defensive positions to keep the British penned in. He was also aware that the initial enlistments issued immediately after Lexington and Concord would expire in December, which meant that Washington would have to begin recruiting and supplying a whole new army. A mountain of problems confronted Washington in the field, and the military situation would be a constant concern for the Congress as they deliberated about what course to take.

MAKE LOVE, NOT WAR

There was also the unanswered question regarding their ties and allegiances to England. George III had spurned the request for reconciliation sent by the First Continental Congress. On July 5, 1775, the Second Congress approved and sent the Olive Branch Petition that appealed to the King to intercede for his colonies against the evil designs of Parliament. The next day, the delegates approved a Declaration of the Causes and Necessity of Taking Up Arms, written by John Dickinson and Thomas Jefferson. Firm, yet conciliatory, the Declaration enumerated the excesses of Parliament over the past eleven years that had left the colonists with no alternative but armed resistance. Yet the Declaration concluded by imploring God to persuade the enemies of the colonies of the justness of their cause so that further violence might be averted. There was still hope that an acceptable peace could be reached. The Congress adjourned at the beginning of August for a few weeks to see what response they might receive and to briefly escape the sweltering Philadelphia summer.

A few weeks later, the Congress reconvened and received their reply from the Crown: King George had issued a Proclamation of Rebellion on August 23, declaring that the colonists were in "open and avowed rebellion" and ordering royal officials in America to move quickly "in the suppression of such rebellion." He then hired 20,000 mercenary soldiers from several German states to help put down rebellion in the colonies. It was clear that an all-out war was inevitable, but many in the Continental Congress were still reluctant to declare independence from England.

PUSH FOR INDEPENDENCE

Events were brewing that would begin to shift opinion towards that option. The belligerent policy of King George and Parliament was a critical factor. Parliament issued the Prohibitory Act in December which declared that all trade with the colonies was prohibited, colonial ships were to be confiscated, and civil government in America was to be replaced with military rule. John Adams declared that George III, by supporting this bill, had broken his covenant with his American subjects. As a covenant-breaker, he was no longer entitled to their loyalty. Still, delegates from Maryland, Pennsylvania, New Jersey, and Delaware were instructed by their state governments to take a moderate course and consider any acceptable measures of reconciliation offered by the Crown.

The military situation took a turn for the worse at the end of 1775. On December 31, the American forces under Montgomery and Arnold attacked Quebec and were defeated. The battle left Montgomery dead and Arnold seriously wounded. In addition, Ethan Allen, who had joined the Canada expedition as a volunteer to recruit Canadians for Montgomery's force, was captured after launching a hasty attack on Montreal with a small force. When the British general realized that his prisoner was the conqueror of Fort Ticonderoga, he had him bound in chains and sent off to England for trial on charges of treason and rebellion.

A day after the defeat at Quebec, Lord Dunmore, the British governor of Virginia, ordered a naval barrage of the town of Norfolk, one of the major trading centers in the state. Late in the night, a British force landed ashore and set fire to the town, killing several citizens. One American military observer related the horrible scene in a dispatch to the Virginia Convention: "I cannot enter into the melancholy consideration of the women and children running through a crowd of shot to get out of the town, some of them with children at their breasts; a few have, I hear, been killed. Does it not call for vengeance, both from God and man?" News of the brutal attack at Norfolk traveled throughout the colonies and galvanized public opinion against the English.

In January of 1776, Thomas Paine, an Englishman who had only been in America two years, published a pamphlet entitled *Common Sense*. A London associate of Ben Franklin, Paine had gained a job as editor of an American magazine. Admiring his writing ability, Franklin encouraged him to write something on the conflict between England and America. Finishing it quickly, he enlisted the help of Benjamin Rush to help get it published.

In three months, 120,000 copies of this electrifying little book had been sold and were being widely circulated. What it said was simple: America was destined to become a great and independent power, but it needed to immediately declare independence to win foreign allies to its cause. Without independence, the conflict was nothing more than a colonial rebellion, and America would never gain support from France and Spain. But even more powerful than the argument was the fiery rhetoric that flowed from Paine's pen: "O ye that love mankind," he wrote, "Ye that dare oppose, not only the tyranny, but the tyrant, stand forth! Every spot of the old world is overrun with oppression. Freedom hath been hunted round the globe. Asia and Africa have long expelled her—Europe regards her like a stranger, and England hath given her warning to depart. O! receive the fugitive, and prepare in time an asylum for mankind."

Paine's popular and forceful style was similar to the sermons of Samuel Davies and the speeches of Patrick Henry. While in favor of independence, John Adams wrote a response criticizing *Common Sense* for its revolutionary tone, which he thought bordered on anarchy. For Adams, Paine's work was "so democratical, without any restraint or even an attempt at any equilibrium or counterpoise, that it must produce confusion and every evil work." But the pamphlet's popularity encouraged George Washington, who wrote to a friend, "I find Common Sense is working a powerful charge in the minds of many men." The appearance of this pamphlet at this time probably helped convince many who were undecided to favor cutting all ties with Great Britain.

PATRIOTS FINALLY ENTER BOSTON

In March 1776, less than a year after the battle of Bunker Hill and Breed's Hill, the Americans seriously threatened the British positions when they placed fifty cannons on Dorchester Heights overlooking Boston Harbor and the British troops. These were some of the same cannons captured the year before by Benedict Arnold and Ethan Allen at Fort Ticonderoga. Colonel Henry Knox had supervised their transport to Boston by building wood sleds and dragging them through the snow for over three hundred miles. General Howe, who took control of the British garrison stationed in Boston in October after George III removed General Gage as commander, realized that he was at a serious disadvantage. He negotiated the withdrawal of his British troops and a thousand Tory citizens in return for not burning the city down. Loading up more than 125 ships, General Howe and the British sailed away from Boston, with the Continental Army, under General Washington's command, now at last in full control of the city.

AMERICAN DEFENSE IN THE SOUTH

In the meantime, General Charles Lee had left Boston with troops to prevent British General Henry Clinton from landing an assault force somewhere in Virginia or the Carolinas. He established a headquarters in Williamsburg awaiting word about where Clinton's force was going to land. As Lee waited in Virginia, a band of North Carolina militia, under the command of Colonel James Moore, confronted fifteen hundred Loyalists troops from the area, who were awaiting Clinton's landing. Taking their stand at Moore's Creek Bridge, the Americans defeated the

Loyalists and broke the back of the British opposition in North Carolina. On March 7, the Americans took control of Hutchinson Island across the river from the Georgia capital of Savannah.

THE ROAD TO INDEPENDENCE

General Washington's bloodless victory at Boston had freed New England from the British threat and strengthened the determination of the Continental Army. It took heart in the valiant defense of the south under General Lee and the state militias. These substantive victories gave the Continental Congress the confidence that the battle against the most powerful nation in the world could be won. The states, struggling to define their political systems while defending their lands from British raids, took notice of the trend.

By the end of March, South Carolina had adopted a temporary constitution, effectively ending British control of the colony. Emboldened by their victory at Moore's Creek Bridge, the Fourth Provincial Congress of North Carolina approved the Halifax Resolves on April 12, instructing their delegates in Philadelphia to "concur with the delegates of the other colonies in declaring independency [...]." This move towards independence in North Carolina had begun almost a year earlier when leaders in Mecklenberg County passed what became known as the Mecklenberg Resolves. The Resolves severed ties with England and proclaimed "that all laws and commissions confirmed by, or derived from the authority of the King or Parliament, are annulled[...]."

On May 15, 1776, the Virginia Convention passed a motion to direct their delegates to propose a resolution to the Continental

Congress that would declare the thirteen colonies free and independent states. The battle had been hard-fought in Virginia between those who favored independence and those who wanted to remain loyal to the crown, but those who wanted independence had become a clear majority. The change was brought about by such men as Patrick Henry, George Mason, James Madison, and Edmund Pendleton who, when elected to the Convention, persuaded it to vote in favor of complete independence and to call for a union of the states to pursue that goal. Rhode Island and Massachusetts quickly followed suit. John Adams encouraged all of the states to take measures to begin to form their own independent governments.

Two days after the vote in Virginia, John Witherspoon, who had assumed a seat in the Continental Congress for New Jersey, preached a fast day sermon at Princeton that encouraged his hearers to take hope in the providence of God despite the circumstances and to acknowledge that God had been protecting the colonies in their struggle for freedom. Apologizing for the political nature of his discourse, he said, "You are all my witnesses, that this is the first time of my introducing any political subject into the pulpit. At this season however, it is not only lawful but necessary, and I willingly embrace the opportunity of declaring my opinion without any hesitation, that the cause in which America is now in arms, is the cause of justice, of liberty, and of human nature."

The pulpits and the pamphlets resounded with the same voice. From the taverns to the meeting halls, from Maine to Georgia, it was clear that the movement to declare independence was afoot.

The Virginia delegation took the lead in Philadelphia when Richard Henry Lee made a motion on June 9, 1776 "that these United Colonies are and of right ought to be free and independent states, that they are absolved from all allegiance to the British Crown, and that all political connection between them and the state of Great Britain is and ought to be totally dissolved." Despite a rash of "independence fever," not all of the members were quite yet convinced. Some additional time was needed to consider the matter. The Continental Congress appointed a committee led by Lee to draw up a Declaration of Independence, should the motion be passed, explaining the reasons why the colonies were taking such a momentous step. Though Lee was almost immediately called away due to his wife's illness, the committee—composed of Thomas Jefferson, Benjamin Franklin, John Adams, Roger Sherman, and Robert R. Livingston—went to work on a draft of the covenant lawsuit.

Additional committees were set up to prepare a plan of confederation that would act as a constitution for the union of states and to establish relations with foreign governments to enlist their support against the British. As the various committees labored on their plans and documents through June 1776, word arrived from the south that British General Clinton and his forces were forced to abandon their plans to invade Charleston after General Lee and his men made a gallant defense of the city. General Clinton had ordered his ships to turn around and sail north to join forces with General Howe.

As July 1 approached, the date set for all the committees to report back and for Congress to vote on their recommendations, excitement was high in Philadelphia and throughout all the states. While there were many details for the Continental Congress to work out regarding the defense of the colonies, the structure of the union of states, and the plan to convince France and Spain to assist the Americans in their cause, the question on everyone's mind was whether the Continental Congress would vote for independence. The world would soon find out.

CHAPTER 11: DAVID VERSUS GOLIATH

"One man with courage makes a majority."

ANDREW JACKSON

The Americans were once again on the threshold of dramatic change. In the two years since the Battles of Lexington and Concord, the colonial leaders struggled with the issue of taking up arms against the British. Now the movement was moving the Continental Congress towards severing all ties with England. As the English increased their military presence in America, they were quickly met and challenged by the colonial militias and the Continental Army, which resulted in escalating the situation all the more. It was now obvious to the members of the Congress that King George wanted nothing less than their complete submission. The state assemblies were becoming more insistent on independence, instructing their delegates to support such measures. Any peace to be won was either at the cost of fighting a protracted war with England or submitting to the domination of King and Parliament. As the debate regarding Richard Henry Lee's motion for independence approached, there was little doubt what road the Americans would take.

DRAFTING THE DECLARATION

In anticipation of the debate, the Congress had appointed various committees to begin to draft a declaration of independence, framing a set of articles for governing the country, and establishing diplomatic ties with foreign allies, most notably the French, Spanish, and Dutch. When the committee drafting the declaration first met, there was a discussion of who would be the first to try to craft a document for the committee to work on. The most obvious choice was John Adams, but he deferred to his younger colleague, Thomas Jefferson. Despite being only thirty-two years old, Jefferson had already established a reputation as a solid writer and thinker with the publication of his pamphlet, *A Summary View of the Rights of British America*. Now he was given the awesome task of composing America's public defense of independence.

When he began his first drafts of the declaration, Jefferson was anxious about events back in Virginia. The Convention was considering a new state constitution, and he wanted to be sure that the new document reflected the political lessons the colonists had learned over the past two decades of conflict with England. Needing some assurance that his views would be made known, he composed a few drafts of his own proposed state constitution and sent them off to Williamsburg. With only a few weeks before the July 1 debate on independence, Jefferson knew that he had to begin to put some of his thoughts to paper.

The first question that Jefferson had to address was the legitimacy of the Congress making a declaration of independence. In the past, the colonists had argued that their resistance was justified because their rights as British citizens had been violated. But in recent years, the apologists for the Crown maintained that as colonists, they could not claim those rights and were subject to whatever rules the King and Parliament created. The Crown had absolute authority, they argued. Jefferson was faced with a second question: who was the audience to whom the declaration was directed? Was it just the King and people back in England? Or was the audience much wider?

Jefferson found one answer to both questions. Rather than relying on British law for their defense, the Americans would appeal to fixed moral standards of the natural law, or the law of nations, to make a worldwide public announcement of their new form of government and defense of their actions. The declaration would be a message to the world and to posterity about the propriety of their defensive actions against the oppressive British Empire.

Jefferson knew that with this approach, he had a lot of history to draw from. Not only were there a number of resolutions, protests, and declarations that were submitted to the British since the Stamp Act crisis over a decade ago, but he could also reach back in time to use the language of the Dutch Declaration of Independence of 1581, when the Dutch Protestants freed themselves from Roman Catholic Spain. The Reformation had also birthed a wealth of political literature, transmitted through the French Huguenots, the Dutch Reformed, the Scottish Covenanters, and the English Puritans, that emphasized the limited and contractual nature of government. Such works, like Samuel

Rutherford's *Lex, Rex* (1644) and the *Vindiciae Contra Tyrannos* (1572), which John Adams stated was a major influence in his political thinking, made the case that when rulers put themselves above the law to violate it, they become felons according to the law and could be resisted. It was from the Reformation that America received its belief in the contractual basis of society.

But not only did he have a good deal of historical precedent to draw on, he had the pattern of covenant lawsuits portrayed all throughout the Old Testament—and especially in the Minor Prophets. If, as the Americans contended, Parliament and Crown had violated their covenantal agreements with their colonies, then the pattern of issuing a covenant lawsuit carried the justification of spiritual faithfulness as well as the justification of political expeditiousness.

There were other points to be made. One of the primary ideas Jefferson wanted to convey was that the Americans were being driven by necessity. The English were bringing troops to America to subdue it by force. They were burning towns and attacking innocent civilians. The Continental Congress had a duty to protect their citizens. It also needed to be made clear that the Americans were not grasping for power—this was not an America *revolution*. Quite to the contrary, they were resisting the revolution of the English that asserted the unlimited powers of King and Parliament over the colonies. Not only had the English violated the terms of the colonial charters, they were infringing on the inalienable rights given by God to all people. Finally, the declaration had to state the level of resolve by the Americans. This had to be a complete and final separation from

England, and the members of the Continental Congress had to affirm their absolute commitment to uphold it.

With these things in mind, Jefferson composed his first few drafts of the declaration. Making some revisions, he submitted it to the committee, where John Adams and Ben Franklin proposed some small alterations. Otherwise, the committee submitted the American Declaration of Independence to the Continental Congress for its review and consideration on June 29.

INDEPENDENCE AT LAST

The day arrived when Congress was scheduled to consider Richard Henry Lee's motion for independence. Jefferson's declaration was read aloud. Many members rose to speak, with the assembly leaning towards independence but still divided. John Dickinson said that time should be given to prepare and approve the articles of government. John Adams rose and gave a passionate defense for declaring independence, yet only nine of the thirteen states were prepared to support Lee's motion. But before retiring for the day, a note arrived from General Washington informing the Congress that he anticipated the British to attack in New York at any moment. Congress agreed to take a vote the next day.

When the matter was taken up that following morning, July 2, 1776, it was clear that South Carolina and New York were now prepared to support the resolution. A vote was called and the motion for independence was approved without a single dissenting vote. But the cautious patriots wanted to be absolutely certain they were taking the right step, so they delayed making their vote public for a few more days.

On July 4, the Congress made some changes that were suggested to the draft declaration, and once approved later that day, the representatives began to sign the covenant. On July 8, Congress ordered that copies of the Declaration of Independence should be made and distributed to the public. Thus, the immortal words resounded:

> We hold these truths to be self-evident: that all men are created equal, that they are endowed by their Creator with certain unalienable rights, that among these are life, liberty and the pursuit of happiness. That to secure these rights, governments are instituted among men, deriving their just powers from the consent of the governed; that whenever any form of government becomes destructive of these ends, it is the right of the people to alter or to abolish it, and to institute new government, laying its foundation on such principles and organizing its powers in such form, as to them shall seem most likely to effect their safety and happiness.

The Declaration documented a train of abuses perpetrated by the British Empire and the attempts by the colonies to resolve the differences through peaceful means. But in the end, it was now clear that the time had come for the United States to take their leave from England. The American states were now free and independent. With a final appeal to Heaven, the Congress concluded the declaration with an unequivocal statement of their commitment: "And for the support of this declaration, with a firm reliance on the protection of Divine Providence, we mutually pledge to each other our lives, our fortunes, and our sacred honor."

As word traveled throughout the states about the signing of the Declaration of Independence, there were celebrations from north to south. But the British were not about to agree so easily. General Washington was trying desperately to hold onto New York, and there were British troops amassing in several states and in Canada to smash the growing rebellion. Now that the Americans had declared their freedom from England, they would have to fight to secure it.

BRITISH STRATEGY FOR VICTORY

Once the fighting had actually begun, the British came up with a three-pronged strategy to put down the rebellion in America. The first part of their strategy was to cut off and isolate the New England colonies from the rest. After all, it was in New England that the Sons of Liberty had been most active in organizing resistance to British authority. If New England could be sealed off, the British authorities reasoned, they could easily defeat resistance in the rest of the colonies.

The second part of British strategy called for recruiting the Loyalists living in the southern colonies. Convinced that there were at least as many, if not more, in these colonies who favored keeping ties with the Crown, the British believed that if they were to send forces in large numbers to the South, they could raise enough troops from among the Loyalists already there to overwhelm the rebel forces.

The third aspect of the royal strategy was simple. With a Loyalist South on one flank and an isolated New England on the other, those Patriots in the Middle Colonies would be cut off from any support and could be readily defeated. One weakness of such a strategy was that for it to work, all three parts of it had to be carried out. If any one part of the plan were to fail, the British troops would themselves be vulnerable to being cut off.

WASHINGTON ON THE RUN

Although Washington tried valiantly to hold on to New York, British General Howe's army made a surprise attack in September 1776 and pursued the Continental Army through New York, up the Hudson River, and into New Jersey. While many men had been lost, Washington was grateful that he still had an army to command. But trapped on the banks of the Delaware River and facing certain destruction, Washington took a gamble that he could move his army across the Delaware River and into Pennsylvania under cover of darkness. Almost miraculously, an unusually dense fog appeared that concealed the American troops' movements. The fog, said many eyewitnesses, was providential, and lifted only after the last of Washington's troops had made it safely across the river.

For good measure, Washington's men had seized all the boats on the river so that the British could not use them in pursuit. The Americans had made a successful retreat, but they were still on the run with only the Delaware River separating them from a British army strong enough to destroy them. A discouraged Commander-in-Chief wrote to his brother Lawrence in December of 1776: "If every nerve is not strained to recruit a new army with all possible expedition, I think the game is nearly up." Strangely, the British did not pursue Washington across the Delaware. General Howe felt that by forcing the Continental Army into the wilderness as winter began to set in, he only had to wait a short time until Washington surrendered.

WASHINGTON STRIKES BACK

While he was temporarily safe from a British assault, Washington faced another pressing problem. At the end of December, the enlistments for many of his troops would expire. He knew something had to be done to rouse the spirits of his men and to encourage them to stay. After his defeat at New York and his hasty retreat into New Jersey and across the Delaware, Washington was aware that there were now critics in Congress calling for his removal.

In a bold and brilliant move, Washington decided to strike the British an unexpected blow. Under cover of a severe snowstorm on Christmas night, 1776, he ordered the entire army to cross the Delaware River. They marched all night towards Trenton, New Jersey, where they were hoping to surprise a garrison of Hessian troops stationed there. One of the officers at Washington's side was a young colonel and a recent graduate of King's College in New York, Alexander Hamilton. Cold and tired, the Americans attacked the Hessians, who tried to hurriedly organize a defense. The Americans overwhelmed them, taking almost a thousand prisoners and needed supplies. The Battle of Trenton proved to be a stirring success for General Washington.

Receiving news of the American victory, General Howe sent General Cornwallis in pursuit of Washington. The American commander played a clever trick on his British foe by ordering his army to build large campfires at night and then to withdraw quietly into the darkness of the woods behind the blazes. Washington then marched his Patriot army on to Princeton where he defeated a British force on January 3, 1777. After this victory, the Continental army went into their winter quarters in Morristown, New Jersey. Word of the victories at Trenton and

Princeton increased enlistments in the Continental Army and many who had Tory leanings came over to the Patriot cause.

TIMES THAT TRY MEN'S SOULS

But it was still a dark time for General Washington. The small victories at Trenton and Princeton boosted American morale, but he had yet to defeat a British army. General Charles Lee, who had defended Charleston and pushed the British out of the South in April 1776, had been appealing to Congress to remove Washington and appoint him as Commander-in-Chief. Stopping in Philadelphia to confer with the Congress while Washington was defending himself in New York, Lee noted to the members of the assembly that he had served in the British Army during the Seven Years' War, while Washington had only commanded a unit of colonial militia. He was clearly more qualified for the position. To emphasize his point and to make Washington's job more difficult, Lee refused to join his troops with Washington's in the midst of the retreat through New York and New Jersey.

Settling down in Morristown, New Jersey in December 1776, while Washington sat on the west side of the Delaware River, Lee decided one night to indulge his lusts by traveling to Basking Ridge, where a woman, Mrs. White, maintained a brothel. Taking up for the night with one of the prostitutes there, General Lee awoke for breakfast to find a troubling surprise—thirty British dragoons had surrounded Mrs. White's house. Without any troops to defend him, Lee promptly surrendered himself to the British troops. He was taken to headquarters and turned over to General Cornwallis. For the moment, Washington's primary competitor was now in British hands.

One man who observed General Washington's travails was Thomas Paine. He had been volunteering his services to the Continental Army and had witnessed the difficult retreat through New Jersey. He determined to defend Washington's cause. Writing a new pamphlet, *The Crisis*, he made the case for the Americans to persevere through these troubled times and events and look forward to their future of freedom. Despite his personal reservations about the Christian faith, Paine expressed a religious-like devotion and he believed Divine Providence would sustain the Patriots and bring success to the American cause. This was no time to despair. As Paine wrote:

> These are the times that try men's souls. The summer soldier and the sunshine patriot will, in this crisis, shrink from the service of his country; but he that stands it now, deserves the love and thanks of man and woman. Tyranny, like hell, is not easily conquered; yet we have this consolation with us, that the harder the conflict, the more glorious the triumph. What we obtain too cheap, we esteem to lightly: 'Tis dearness only that gives everything its value. Heaven knows how to put a proper price upon its goods; and it would be strange indeed if so celestial an article as Freedom should not be highly rated.

Paine's piece had a stirring effect. Many soldiers continued to reenlist. Washington received some additional assistance from his friend, Robert Morris, a Philadelphia banker, who responded to an urgent call from General Washington to provide enough money to give bonuses to the men who extended their enlistments. Morris generously replied and kept the hopes for winning the war alive during the winter of 1776-1777. The fires of freedom were still burning.

SARATOGA

During the next year, Americans would need some hope and some divine intervention to prevent the British from destroying the Continental Army. As determined as ever to carry out their strategy, the British made their plans for the Spring of 1777. An army under the command of General John Burgoyne would march southward from Montreal, sail down Lake Champlain, retake Forts Crown Point and Ticonderoga, occupy Saratoga, and proceed to Albany, the colonial capital of New York. There Burgoyne would rendezvous with British armies under the command of General Henry Clinton and General Barry St. Leger. The plan called for St. Leger's forces to move in a southwesterly direction from Montreal down the St. Lawrence River, sail down the eastern portion of Lake Ontario, disembark at Fort Oswego, and then proceed along the Mohawk River to Oriskany, Fort Stanwix, and on to Albany. Meanwhile, General Clinton's forces would march northward from New York City along the Hudson to meet the armies of St. Leger and Burgoyne. If all had gone as planned, this would have effectively cut off and isolated New England and ensured the success of the first part of the British strategy.

But the campaign was a disaster for the British. General St. Leger, moving from the west, was met and defeated at the Battle of Oriskany by General Nicholas Herkimer, well short of his goal of Albany. General Clinton's forces made it only halfway the distance from New York City to Albany. American General Horatio Gates marched northwards from Albany to engage General John Burgoyne. The two armies met at the Battle of Saratoga.

When the two sides collided, the Americans badly beat the outnumbered British troops. Burgoyne attempted to lead his men away from the field, but Gates continued to harass the Redcoats with artillery and sniper fire. Confronted by superior numbers and with no word on General Clinton's reinforcements, Burgoyne arranged for the surrender of his five thousand troops to Gates on October 17, 1777. Saratoga was a tremendous victory for the American cause. Colonel Benedict Arnold, who had defeated Burgoyne in the opening battle but had suffered a broken leg during the fighting, played a vital role in Gates' victory.

FROM PEAK TO VALLEY

Meanwhile, General Howe headed for Philadelphia in an effort to capture the infant nation's capital city. Washington's forces tried to stop him at the Battles of Brandywine and Germantown in September but were defeated. By year's end in 1777, Howe was solidly in control of Philadelphia and a discouraged Continental Army made its way a few miles north to winter quarters in Valley Forge.

The Valley Forge bivouac, in the terrible winter of 1777-78, was the low point for Washington and his army. Their defeats in the preceding months stung American confidence. Washington also had to contend with a new competitor for his position as Commander-in-Chief, General Gates. After a spectacular win at Saratoga, Gates was very popular with the members of Congress. Since Washington's appointment, many of the members that had voted for him earlier had left the Congress to assist in setting up the state governments. Some of the powerful men who remained, including John Adams, were openly supporting Gates. Congress had also appointed another

Washington critic, Thomas Conway, as Inspector General for the Continental Army.

Washington also had to fight his own people. Many farmers in the Valley Forge area had sold their livestock and harvests to the British, who were camped for the winter in nearby Philadelphia. Unlike Washington, the British could pay in hard currency. Meanwhile, the soldiers of the Continental Army barely ate enough to survive the harsh winter.

Private James Martin wrote about the suffering of these men in his diary:

> The army was now not only starved but naked; the greatest part were not only shirtless and barefoot, but destitute of all other clothing, especially blankets. I procured a small piece of raw cowhide and made myself a pair of moccasins, which (while they lasted) kept my feet from the frozen ground, although, as I well remember, the hard edges so galled my ankles, while on a march, that it was with much difficulty and pain that I could wear them afterwards; but the only alternative I had was to endure this inconvenience or to go barefoot, as hundreds of my companions had to, till they might be tracked by their blood upon the rough frozen ground.

Despite the deprivations, Washington's men looked to him for encouragement. They kept their spirits high—at least as high as possible in the deplorable conditions. They were still free, and the hope of a victory was not yet lost. The Americans had demonstrated that at the Battle of Saratoga. Those who didn't believe in General Washington had long since left for home. The men who survived the winter at Valley Forge knew the price they had to pay for liberty and looked forward to the opportunity of challenging the British troops when the weather warmed. They did their best to keep themselves and the dream of an independent United States alive.

CHAPTER 12: VALLEY TO VICTORY

"The highest glory of the American Revolution was this; it connected in one indissoluble bond, the principles of the civil government with the principles of Christianity. From the day of the Declaration the American people were bound by the laws of God, which they all, and by the laws of the Gospel, which they nearly all, acknowledged as the rules of their conduct."

JOHN QUINCY ADAMS

While the Continental Army was camped at Valley Forge and the British Army under General Howe was enjoying all the pleasures that Philadelphia had to offer, events overseas would change the course of the war. After the signing of the Declaration of Independence, the Committee of Secret Correspondence, the foreign affairs committee of the Continental Congress, had authorized for three Americans, Ben Franklin, Silas Deane and Arthur Lee (Richard Henry Lee's brother), to represent the United States in France and, hopefully, to forge a military and commercial alliance to further shift the tide of the war towards the American cause.

Having declared independence and seen victory at the Battle of Saratoga under General Gates, the American diplomatic mission gained some bargaining chips. General Burgoyne's failure to cut off New England meant the collapse of the other two parts of their strategy for subduing America. But more importantly, it demonstrated to the French that the Americans had a fighting chance to win the war. Having been sorely defeated by the British in the French and Indian War and having lost Canada and other territories as the result, the French were eager for revenge against their hated enemy. But they were not willing to risk fighting the British again unless they had a real chance of victory. Saratoga convinced them that they had a real chance to carve up the British Empire. Guided by Benjamin Franklin's brilliant diplomacy, they soon made a treaty of friendship and commerce with the Americans, which led directly to an outright military agreement. The Treaty of Alliance between France and America was signed in Paris in February 1778. France was now in the war on the side of the Americans.

Another direct benefit from the international diplomatic efforts was the arrival of several foreign military officers to assist the Continental Army. One of the first to arrive was the Marquis de Lafayette from France in August 1777. Receiving an appointment as a major general, he was assigned to General Washington's command and quickly become a trusted friend and reliable commander. Another valuable foreign asset was Baron Friedrich Wilhelm Augustus von Steuben, who had served as an officer in Frederick the Great's Prussian army years earlier. He, too, was assigned to

General Washington and arrived in the Valley Forge camp to begin to train the Continental Army as professional soldiers.

POLITICS AS USUAL

Washington received the foreign military assistance just as several competitors for his position of Commander-in-Chief began their efforts to have him removed from command. The challengers tried to use several changes in the Congress to their advantage. First was a change in leadership. John Hancock had resigned as President to return to Massachusetts to help shape the new state government. Henry Laurens of South Carolina was then elected as the new President. The second was the establishment of a Board of War to oversee the operations of the Continental Army. Fresh from his victory at Saratoga, General Gates had been appointed president of the Board, along with General Thomas Mifflin and Colonel Timothy Pickering, both of whom favored replacing Washington with Gates. Another Washington critic, General Thomas Conway, was promoted to major general and received an appointment as Inspector General of the Army. Washington's enemies now held official positions that could threaten his command.

The political plot went awry when letters exchanged between Conway and Gates were sent by the angry Commander-in-Chief to Congress, which caused considerable embarrassment to Conway. President Laurens quickly expressed his strong support for Washington and his leadership of the Continental Army. Washington also fired off a fiery rebuke to General Gates for his involvement in the plan to oust him. The whole crew was promptly discredited when the Board of War, headed by General

Gates, devised to send Conway and Lafayette on a mission to Canada, which quickly fell apart and damaged the reputations of all those involved in the "Conway Cabal." With the political intrigue fully behind him, Washington could now devote his full attention to the war effort.

ALONE NO MORE

By now, British Prime Minister Lord North knew he had a new enemy: France. In early 1778, he sent word to Congress signifying his government's willingness to compromise on every point that the colonies had made since 1765, if only they would lay down their arms, but it was too late. In 1779, Spain and Holland joined the fight against England. The Spanish monarchy, however, wanted nothing to do with revolutionaries and officially allied itself only with France, not with the Americans.

The French immediately dispatched a fleet of twelve warships with several regiments of fully equipped troops on board. They were destined for Delaware Bay, where they would threaten the British troops stationed in Philadelphia. General Sir Henry Clinton, who had replaced Howe as head of the British forces in America, was ordered to evacuate his troops by boat to New York. But because there was not enough room for all his troops as well as the Philadelphia Loyalists who wanted to accompany them, Clinton disobeyed his orders. On June 18, he set off on foot through the New Jersey countryside toward New York.

Soon after, Washington led his army out of Valley Forge in pursuit of the retreating Redcoats. Though he wanted a full-scale battle, his staff felt that this might bring disaster. Washington compromised by sending a force to attack Clinton's slow-moving baggage train. However, Clinton surprised the Americans and swung around with a superior force at Monmouth Courthouse. The Americans broke into a retreat until Washington rode to the front, restored order, and beat off two British attacks. Both armies that day suffered about three hundred casualties. The British army made it safely to New York City, baggage train and all, where they occupied the city and held it for the remainder of the war. The best that Washington could manage in the north was a stalemate.

WAR WHOOPS IN THE WEST

Most Indians sided with the British during the war. Early in 1778, the British lieutenant governor of Detroit, Colonel Henry Hamilton, known as "Hair-buyer Hamilton" for his practice of paying Indians for American scalps, launched Indian scalping parties on a series of raids throughout Ohio, Illinois, and Kentucky. One such raid captured the famous trailblazer Daniel Boone.

The Patriots fought back. George Rogers Clark, sometimes called the "Washington of the West" for his strategy to secure the frontier, sent out spies. They returned with news that the western Indians had no strong loyalty to the British. Clark then appealed to Governor Patrick Henry and other Virginia leaders to send him with a detachment of troops into the western lands claimed by Virginia. His argument that "if a country is not worth protecting, it is not worth claiming" proved persuasive. Virginia could spare only 175 men, but it was enough. Clark marched west in the summer of 1778 and easily took the surprised British forces at Forts Kaskaskia, Cahokia, and Vincennes in southern Illinois and Indiana.

Fearful that Clark's victories might cause the Indians to doubt the value of their alliance with the British, "Hair-buyer" Hamilton recaptured Vincennes in December. When Clark learned of this setback, he began a mid-winter march of over two hundred miles, during which he and his men sometimes had to wade waist-deep in icy water. In February of 1779, the astonished Hamilton found himself besieged by Virginia frontiersmen. He quickly surrendered. Clark brought the "Hair-buyer" back with him to Virginia where Hamilton spent the rest of the war in a Williamsburg prison. George Rogers Clark had broken the power of the British in the West. His victories paved the way for British recognition of the American claims to the area in the peace treaty that ended the War of Independence. Even so, Clark and his men never received so much as a penny in pay either from Virginia, which sponsored his raids, or from Congress.

THE WAR MOVES SOUTH

By the end of 1778, the British had shifted their focus to the South. They were convinced that there were many Loyalists there who would, under the right circumstances, take up arms against the Patriots. Success crowned the first British efforts in the South. In December, they took Savannah and soon extended their control throughout most of Georgia. In October 1779, the Patriots fought back. Joined by the French fleet, they laid siege to Savannah and planned to attack. But a deserter had alerted the British to the plans. When the Patriots attacked, some eight hundred of them were killed or wounded. The Polish nobleman Count Pulaski, who served the Patriot cause as a cavalry commander, was killed. The commander of the French fleet that had arrived to support the Continental Army, Admiral D'Estaing, was wounded and promptly took his fleet back to France.

Back in New York, General Clinton then decided to stage a full-scale invasion of the South. He took nearly eight thousand troops with him and laid siege for three months to Charleston, South Carolina. In May of 1780, Charleston fell. Clinton took over five thousand prisoners, including three generals. The rest of South Carolina was easily captured following this disaster. Clinton sensed total victory was in his grasp and set off for New York to try to finish off Washington's army. He left General Charles Cornwallis in command of British forces in the South. Cornwallis promptly began a major effort to defeat the Patriots and set up loyalist governments.

Faced with a serious crisis, Congress recalled General Gates from retirement and sent him south. Gates planned a surprise attack on British troops near Camden, South Carolina, in August of 1780. Unfortunately, the British planned a surprise attack of their own. The two armies met on the road at two in the morning and began to fight at daybreak. When the fighting was over, the Americans had lost their second army in less than four months.

Following this defeat, Gates was replaced by General Nathanael Greene. He was considered by many to be the best American commander, next to Washington. A number of American Tories, who had earlier supported the Loyalists, recoiled from British destruction of their farms and property and embraced the Patriot cause. During the troubled period after the defeat of General Gates at Camden and before General Greene could regroup American forces in the South, Patriot citizen resistance harried the British, destroyed their supplies, and gave them false information. Francis

Marion, the Swamp Fox, headed a band of guerrilla fighters who kept up a constant harassment of British forces and simply disappeared into the swamps when the British pursued them.

As Cornwallis moved north expecting to easily capture North Carolina, he sent out a detachment under Major Patrick Ferguson to clear the piedmont area on the way. Nine hundred mountain men from the east Tennessee settlement of Watauga trapped Ferguson atop King's Mountain, on the border between North and South Carolina. They killed, wounded, or captured more than a thousand Redcoats, buying time for General Greene and his officers to organize an effective southern campaign. This proved to be a key turning point of the war in the South.

By now, Greene had taken command in the South. Like Washington, he believed that his duty was not so much to win battles but to keep his army together in the field to threaten and harass the enemy. He sought to avoid all unnecessary risks and do battle only when he had a clear advantage. Nevertheless, Greene did take a major gamble by dividing his small army into two, giving the command of one force to Daniel Morgan. Cornwallis responded by sending a thousand of his men after Morgan.

The two armies met at Hannah's Cowpens, a cattle corral by the Broad River on the border of the Carolinas. When the smoke cleared, the Battle of Cowpens had cost the British nine hundred casualties, nine-tenths of their attacking force. Morgan lost a mere handful.

Though Cornwallis called the disaster at Cowpens a "very unexpected and severe blow," he continued to pursue Greene into North Carolina. Greene decided to use strategy rather than challenge the Redcoats in open battle. By repeated, swift strikes followed by quick retreats, Greene lured Cornwallis further and further away from his sources of supply. All the while Greene's army continued to grow. On March 14, he decided to stand his ground near Guilford Courthouse. The battle that followed was technically a British victory because Greene withdrew, leaving Cornwallis in control of the battlefield. But Cornwallis' casualties were much heavier than Greene's, and Greene's army was still together and able to do battle. Cornwallis had failed.

Two days after the battle of Guilford Courthouse, Cornwallis retreated to the coastal city of Wilmington where he could be supplied by ship. By the summer of 1781, only that city and the coastal cities of Savannah and Charleston remained firmly under British control.

TREASON AND TREACHERY

The Continental Army, fighting in the South, faced a new, but familiar enemy. The former American General, Benedict Arnold, had betrayed his country and was serving as a Brigadier General in the South for the British Army under Cornwallis. But his treachery extended further than just changing sides. As early as May 1779, Arnold began communicating with the British side, offering to sell out the Americans while serving as the military commander of Philadelphia. In tribute to his patriotism and because of the war wounds he had received in Quebec and Saratoga fighting for the American cause, General Washington had appointed him commander of the strategic position at West Point, New York, along the Hudson River.

In September 1780, Washington and Lafayette were traveling by West Point and decided to inspect the fort. Upon their arrival,

Arnold was nowhere to be found. After inspecting the fort and finding it in poor condition, Alexander Hamilton handed General Washington some papers captured the day before from a British spy. They revealed a plot by Arnold to surrender the fort at West Point to the British, but by the time Washington was made aware of it, Benedict Arnold had escaped.

But his accomplice, British Major John André, wasn't so fortunate. He was the spy that some local militia members had captured the day before. André hoped to be treated as a prisoner of war because he knew the price of spying—death by hanging. He questioned his guard, Major Benjamin Tallmadge, about how he was to be treated. Major Tallmadge then told André about a close friend who had served General Washington but had been captured and hung as a spy. Tallmadge's friend was the Patriot Nathan Hale. Major André was now to share his fate. After a trial and attempts by General Clinton to negotiate a prisoner exchange for André, General Washington gave the order for him to be hanged. Major André paid with his life, but Benedict Arnold had escaped and was leading raids against the Americans in Virginia. But Arnold's hopes rested with a British victory in the war.

CORNWALLIS CORRALLED

From his base in Wilmington, North Carolina, Lord Cornwallis decided to invade Virginia in the summer of 1781. It seemed like a good plan to him. General Clinton was not happy with the idea because he feared Cornwallis could get trapped between Patriot armies coming from the south and north. Washington, like Clinton, had been preparing for a major battle in the north but sensed a possible opportunity to defeat Cornwallis in Virginia.

He was not yet ready to commit his main army to Virginia, but he did send Lafayette with twelve hundred Continentals—regular army soldiers—and the promise of reinforcements if they were needed. Lafayette, like Greene, had learned his tactics well from Washington. Like Greene, he made surprise raids with his men and quickly fled before Cornwallis, who outnumbered him six to one, could bring up enough troops to strike back.

When Lafayette's reinforcements began to arrive, Cornwallis began to retreat. Clinton then ordered Cornwallis to take up a defensive position along the coast and send part of his army to New York to join Clinton in a new campaign against Philadelphia. The key to this new strategy was the British fleet, which could rescue Cornwallis' army from a trap or send him reinforcements. Unfortunately for Clinton, it had unexpectedly taken off after some French ships. Cornwallis was in a tight situation, and Washington decided the time was ripe to strike.

By now, Lafayette had five thousand Continentals under his command. Several thousand more French troops under the command of Comte de Rochambeau had joined him. Washington and Rochambeau urged the new French admiral, Comte de Grasse, to bring his fleet up from the West Indies to block off any attempt by Cornwallis to escape by sea. When word reached him that de Grasse, thirty ships, and three thousand French marines were on their way, Washington dashed south with his own army to help spring the trap.

On September 28, Washington's 5,700 Continentals and 3,100 militia, along with Rochambeau's 7,000 French troops, and the fleet of Comte de Grasse, laid siege to Cornwallis who was penned in on Virginia's Yorktown Peninsula. The siege continued for three weeks. On October 17, 1781, four years to the day after Burgoyne surrendered at Saratoga, Cornwallis surrendered at Yorktown. At no time during the siege had Cornwallis seriously tried to break out. Moreover, he still had a week of supplies remaining when he gave up. If he had held on a little longer, the British fleet might have saved him, for it arrived four days after the surrender.

During the formal surrender ceremony, the British band played several American and French airs, but their most remembered tune was *The World Turned Upside Down*. Word of the American victory reached the Continental Congress days later, and they responded by adjourning to a nearby Lutheran church to offer prayers of thanksgiving led by an Army chaplain. The leading members of the Pennsylvania government joined the members of Congress in the worship service. President Thomas McKean wrote a note of thanks and congratulations on behalf of the American people to General Washington. When the British Prime Minister, Lord North, received word of Washington's victory at Yorktown, he exclaimed, "Oh, God! It is all over."

The loss of Cornwallis and his army at Yorktown did not mean that the Redcoats were defeated. However, the capture of Cornwallis at Yorktown did reinforce the growing conviction in England that the war was a dangerous waste of Britain's resources. When Lord North resigned, he was replaced by the Earl of Shelburne, who was quite eager to revive good relations with America and sent a representative to Paris to begin negotiations with the Americans for an end to the war.

Meanwhile, General Washington began to make preparations to personally drive the English troops off American soil. In New

York, General Clinton knew that the battle, and the war, was lost. He could not launch an effective campaign in either the North or the South, and the presence of the French fleet dashed any hope of victory. Plans were made to evacuate the British from New York, Savannah, and Charleston under General Guy Carleton. It would take more than two years for the British to leave America entirely, but finally, on November 25, 1783, the last of the British troops evacuated New York City, and General Washington rode down Broadway in triumph.

ANOTHER KING GEORGE?

There was one formidable task left to Washington after the British defeat. Many of his soldiers had not been paid in months, and there were petitions sent to Congress from officers of the Continental Army demanding payment. Riots broke out, and Congress had to move their proceedings from Philadelphia to Princeton, New Jersey to avoid the violence. An aide to General Gates, John Armstrong, Jr., authored a series of anonymous threats to Congress, called the Newburgh Addresses, stating that the army would not fight if engaged and would not disband if Congress commanded it.

To avoid all an all-out mutiny, General Washington convened a meeting of his officers to denounce the Addresses and riots as dishonorable and treasonous. He assured them on the basis of his own integrity that Congress would make good on their promises. He rebuffed their pleas to take control of the government—some of the men even pleading for him to take the crown as the sovereign of the new land. His officers, all of whom had served with Washington for years, were moved to tears by the great man's fealty, and they too swore their allegiance to Congress. The tense situation was finally resolved when Congress authorized full payment to be made to the soldiers over a five-year period.

THE AMERICAN CINCINNATUS

With that, Washington had fought his last battle of the War for Independence. In April 1783, Congress declared the war officially over. The soldiers were furloughed over the next few months, and the Continental Army disbanded. On October 18, 1783, Washington issued his final General Order to the Army, bidding his men a fond farewell. In early December, he gathered with his officers in New York City one last time for dinner. In an evening filled with heavy emotion, he expressed his sincere thanks for their service and friendship and proposed a toast: "With a heart full of love and gratitude, I now take leave of you. I most devoutly wish that your latter days may be as prosperous and happy as your former ones have been glorious and noble." The following day, he left New York for Annapolis, where Congress was now meeting.

On December 23, 1783, Washington entered the Maryland State House. Congress was waiting there for him to arrive. After Washington had been escorted into the chamber, President Thomas Mifflin, who had once been suspected of being part of the Conway Cabal to replace Washington as Commander-in-Chief, now asked the General to address the members of Congress. The room grew hushed, knowing what was about to transpire. Washington congratulated the Congress on the victory in the war and said that he was resigning his commission now that the country had achieved its sovereignty and independence. Asking Congress to take care of his officers, he concluded his short speech, saying:

> I consider it an indispensable duty to close this last solemn act of my Official life, by commending the Interests of our dearest Country to the protection of Almighty God, and those who have the superintendence of them, to his holy keeping. Having now finished the work assigned me, I retire from the great theatre of Action; and bidding an Affectionate farewell to this August body under whose orders I have so long acted, I here offer my Commission, and take my leave of all the employments of public life.

With that, he reached into his pocket and surrendered his commission to President Mifflin, who offered a few words of thanks composed for him by Thomas Jefferson. One observer, James McHenry, said, "The spectators all wept, and there was hardly a member of Congress who did not drop tears."

Like the Roman general Cincinnatus, who refused to seize power after a stunning victory and chose instead to return home to tend his crops, George Washington left the Congress behind and rode off to Mount Vernon, where he would retire with his wife, Martha, to life as a private citizen.

With victory won and the United States now independent and free, the American Cincinnatus was finally going home.

DIVE DEEPER: KING'S MOUNTAIN

One of the great pioneer preachers, Samuel Doak, seemed to have a knack for being at the right place at the right time. A Scotch-Irish Presbyterian, he founded the first church west of the Allegheny Mountains. He traveled with the earliest pioneers of the western frontier into the Watauga Settlement—one of the first communities established on the west side of the Appalachian Mountains. He ministered among them, planting churches, training and discipling young men and women, and offering counsel to the leaders of what would ultimately become the fledgling State of Franklin. Perhaps his greatest legacy was that he founded the first educational institution in the west—which ultimately became Washington College and was the impetus behind the establishment of the University of Tennessee.

But he was also present at the Battle of King's Mountain in 1780—a significant turning point in the American War for Independence and the only battle in the war fought in what is now Tennessee.

The Over-Mountain men, as they were called, gathered at Sycamore Shoals beginning on September 26, 1780 to strategize and organize for their fight against the British loyalist forces, which would occur two weeks later at King's Mountain. Doak preached a sermon to the ragtag army of Patriot farmers and frontiersmen to remind them of what they were fighting for:

> My countrymen, you are about to set out on an expedition which is full of hardships and dangers, but one in which the Almighty will attend you. The Mother Country has her hands upon you, these American colonies, and takes that for which our fathers planted their homes in the wilderness—OUR LIBERTY.

> Taxation without representation and the quartering of soldiers in the homes of our people without their consent are evidence that the Crown of England would take from its American subjects the last vestige of freedom. Your brethren across the mountains are crying like Macedonia unto your help. God forbid that you shall refuse to hear and answer their call—but the call of your brethren is not all. The enemy is marching hither to destroy your homes.

> Brave men, you are not unacquainted with battle. Your hands have already been taught to war and your fingers to fight. You have wrested these beautiful valleys of the Holston and Watauga from the savage hand. Will you tarry now until the other enemy carries fire and sword to your very doors? NO, it shall not be. Go forth then in the strength of your manhood to the aid of your brethren, the defense of your liberty and the protection of your homes. And may the God of justice be with you and give you victory.

> Let us pray: Almighty and gracious God! Thou hast been the refuge and strength of Thy people in all ages. In time of sorest need we have learned to come to Thee—our Rock and our Fortress. Thou knowest the dangers and snares that surround us on march and in battle. Thou knowest the dangers that constantly threaten the humble, but well beloved homes, which Thy servants have left behind them.

O, in Thine infinite mercy, save us from the cruel hand of the savage, and of tyrant. Save the unprotected homes while fathers and husbands and sons are far away fighting for freedom and helping the oppressed. Thou, who promised to protect the sparrow in its flight, keep ceaseless watch, by day and by night, over our loved ones. The helpless woman and little children, we commit to Thy care. Thou wilt not leave them or forsake them in times of loneliness and anxiety and terror.

O, God of Battle, arise in Thy might. Avenge the slaughter of Thy people. Confound those who plot for our destruction. Crown this mighty effort with victory, and smite those who exalt themselves against liberty and justice and truth. Help us as good soldiers to wield the SWORD OF THE LORD AND GIDEON. Amen.

The victory the men were stirred on toward would be one of the most significant in the Southern theater of the War for Independence and virtually assured General Washington's eventual triumph at Yorktown.

CHAPTER 13: WARTIME GOVERNANCE

"No human society has ever been able to maintain both order and freedom, both cohesiveness and liberty apart from the moral precepts of the Christian Religion applied and accepted by all the classes. Should our Republic ever forget this fundamental precept of governance, men are certain to shed their responsibilities for licentiousness and this great experiment will then surely be doomed."

JOHN JAY

The presence of the French fleet in Chesapeake Bay during the siege of Yorktown in 1781 was the result of some sophisticated diplomacy by the struggling American nation. The military success of the British over the previous century, and the hatred that it bred, contributed to an international movement against England. As the war progressed, it became clear that the American War for Independence was more than a domestic dispute between Great Britain and her colonies; the new-world claims of many of the old-world countries—France and Spain in particular—turned the conflict into a world war.

Cornwallis had been cornered and the war had been won with the assistance of France, but this was the fruit of years of efforts by the congressional commissioners in Paris to woo King Louis XVI to the side of the American cause. John Adams had also convinced the Dutch to enter the war by declaring war on Britain and had arranged for a loan in June of 1782—a critical period in the peace negotiations—of five million guilders for the United States. British ships were also subject to attack and confiscation in the Caribbean by Spanish profiteers. But as the peace treaty negotiations wore on, there was considerable intervention in the discussions between America and England by other countries trying to advance their own positions. America was now a full player, and potentially a victim, in European politics, and they needed an experienced team to defend America's interests.

The diplomatic efforts by the Continental Congress began in 1776 when the Committee for Secret Correspondence was established to open up dialogue with foreign countries to enlist their support for American independence. The first team of American commissioners, Ben Franklin, Arthur Lee, and Silas Deane, arrived in Paris to begin negotiations with England's European enemies. Troubles on the American side began almost immediately, as Arthur Lee exasperated the other two commissioners by his quarrelsome demeanor. The French diplomats noticed Lee's temperament as well, but he was supported by a large number of delegates in the Continental Congress. In 1778, hostilities amongst the American commissioners boiled over, and as a result of a campaign by Lee's friends in Congress to have him removed, Silas Deane was recalled to America. He was replaced by John Adams, who quickly noted in his diary upon his arrival in Paris about the conflicts between all the members of the commission and wrote to his friend, James Warren, that Franklin's overwhelming concern for his popularity with the French outweighed the concern for his duties to America. With Adams in Paris, the tensions were diffused, and the commissioners were able to secure the military and financial assistance of France.

Spain was also mindful of the events in the New World. Suspicious of American intent on Spanish claims along the Mississippi River and in Florida, they never fully allied with America but joined the conflict on the side of the French. The New York lawyer, John Jay, was sent to Madrid by Congress in 1780 to negotiate the dispute. He wrote to Samuel Huntington, then President of the Congress, upon his arrival in May 1780 with his assessment of Spanish feelings towards the American cause: "The King and Ministry are warm, yet I have reason to believe that the bulk of the nation is cold toward us. They appear to me to like the English, hate the French, and to have prejudices against us." Those prejudices eventually became too much for Jay to overcome, and the Spanish, who were protective of their New World claims, never fully entered the war.

Having settled the disputes in Paris amongst the American commissioners, John Adams was dispatched by Congress to The Hague for discussions with the Dutch. Their interest was maintaining the profitable chain of trade with America that challenged the British naval blockade, with much of the pressure to come in on the American side rising from the Amsterdam merchants and bankers who benefited from the exchange of contraband. The Dutch government, initially resistant to join the Americans against the British, changed their minds when England declared war on The Netherlands. England claimed that the Dutch violated an earlier peace treaty after Henry Laurens, a former President of Congress and an American diplomat, was apprehended by the British navy with correspondence between the two countries indicating that the Dutch were about to enter the American conflict. Ignoring the claims of diplomatic immunity, Laurens would spend the next year imprisoned in the Tower of London and would be released in exchange for Lord Cornwallis after the British defeat at Yorktown.

One final diplomatic maneuver helped turn the international tide against England. In February 1780, Catherine the Great of Russia established the League of Armed Neutrality with Sweden and Denmark to close off the Baltic Sea to British ships that were searching for arms heading towards America. Over the next two years, Prussia, Portugal, Austria, and the Kingdom of the Two Sicilies joined the alliance. Even the Emperor of Morocco enlisted with the Americans. After years of long, hard efforts by the congressional commissioners stationed around Europe, American diplomacy had effectively isolated England on the international stage.

REINVENTING GOVERNMENT

While America was coordinating their sophisticated negotiations overseas in support of their cause immediately after the signing of the Declaration of Independence, the states had to consider what form of government to adopt now that they were no longer under royal authority. Congress had passed a resolution in May

1776 calling for the states to "adopt such government as shall, in the opinion of the representatives of the people, best conduce to the happiness and safety of their constituents in particular, and America in general."

This was a dire need, as all of the states except Massachusetts, Connecticut, and Rhode Island had never had constitutions and were governed only by tradition and custom administered by the royal governors. The colonial governments under British rule relied on royal appointees and on the King's courts for administration of justice. Once the United States had separated from England and declared their independence, that was all gone, and the states, fresh from the conflicts between royal governors and elected colonial assemblies, kept the lessons of those early battles in mind as they drafted new state governments.

CHECKS AND BALANCES

Two important innovations emerged from this process that are reflected in American government today. An underlying principle of the people investing their own power in the government, rather than being derived from the king, lay at the foundations of both. The first was the direct election by the people for governmental positions that had originally been appointed by the Crown. Furthermore, all hereditary titles were abolished. Thus, all the trappings of monarchy were dropped from the state governments. American citizens, for the first time, had a voice not only in who represented them in the assemblies, but also in who administered the government and the laws.

The second American innovation was the creation of a second legislative body, generally under the title of senate or council, which served as a check on the larger representative bodies. The Americans were concerned about investing any one body of men with an inordinate amount of legislative power. Now, both houses of the legislature had to give their assent to new laws before they were enacted. Eleven of the thirteen colonies adopted the bicameral legislature, with Georgia and Pennsylvania retaining unicameral legislatures.

The immediate question that arose was whether the people would elect the members of the state senates. Ten of the eleven states with bicameral systems provided for popular elections of both houses. Maryland, on the other hand, established a senate composed of fifteen men, nine from the western part of the state, and six from the east side of Chesapeake Bay, who were selected by two electors from each county. These were to be men of influence and restraint that would serve as a real check on the powers of the larger representative and popularly elected assembly.

While Pennsylvania did not adopt a senate into its new form of government, it did create a provision for all bills in the legislature to be published before the bills could be passed into law to allow for the people to make their voices heard to their representatives. It was hoped this would give the people a more direct influence in the affairs of their state government. Another institution incorporated in Pennsylvania's new state constitution was the establishment of a council of censors, who were chosen every seven years and were charged to ensure that the state constitution was being followed by both the executive and legislative branches.

The creation of the censors in Pennsylvania reflected the unwillingness of the people to put too much power in the hands of one man or one government body. While all the states retained the position of governor, all but New York required the governor to share power with an executive council. The state governors were elected either directly by the people, as was the case in New England and New York, or by the legislatures. In New York, the governor also headed a council of revision, which could reject a new law and send it back to the legislature, which could approve the legislation only with the approval of two-thirds of each legislative house. Similar power was given directly to the governor of Massachusetts. This began the American tradition of an executive veto to curb the powers of the state legislatures.

An additional check on both the executive and legislative branches of the new state constitutions was the requirement of office rotation and regular elections for all positions. In many states, one person could not hold executive and legislative offices for extend periods of time, and frequent elections ensured that the people could remove unpopular or corrupt officials in a timely manner. Again, these provisions were intended to keep power from being concentrated in a few hands.

RIGHTS AND WRONGS

To empower the people even further in the face of governmental power, two of the most important states in the new union, Massachusetts and Virginia, established as part of their new constitutions a list of rights guaranteed to every citizen. The Virginia Declaration of Rights, authored by George Mason and passed in May 1776, and the Massachusetts Bill of Rights, authored by John Adams and made the law of the land in 1780, served as worthy successors to the ancient Magna Carta and the 1688 Bill of Rights in England and the Massachusetts Body of Liberties of

1641 and the Pennsylvania Charter of Liberties of 1701. These two constitutional documents secured the civil liberties of citizens by listing in detail the political and judicial rights of protection against improper or unlawful acts of government and by defining the fundamental end of government as preserving and protecting the lives of the people through lawful administration of justice. As the war continued, many states copied the example of Virginia and Massachusetts and attached lists of guaranteed liberties to their own constitutions.

One final feature of the new state constitutions after the Declaration of Independence was their concern for religious liberty. Many states incorporated provisions affirming the duty of everyone to render obedience to their Creator and guaranteeing the right of all citizens to worship God in the manner of their own choosing. With the Anglican Church still making their Loyalist presence felt in many states during the course of the War for Independence, several states disestablished their state-supported churches and began comprehensive public support of religious efforts of all major denominations, with only Rhode Island prohibiting state support for religious activities. Most state constitutions instituted oaths requiring all government officials to profess belief in the Trinity and the Old and New Testaments as God's divine revelation. While the Enlightenment began to chip away at the political recognition of Christianity in the years ahead, with Thomas Jefferson's Virginia Statue of Religious Freedom, passed in January 1786, being the most prominent attempt to detach the Christian religion from the state, America as a whole continued to hold onto its deep Christian roots and maintained the direct connection between Christianity and the political freedoms that the Americans were fighting for.

FEDERAL QUESTIONS

As the states struggled to define their new political systems, the Continental Congress was facing a similar problem. When the thirteen colonies declared their independence, the exact shape of the union of the states was still far from a settled issue. The primary question concerned what powers the new national government would hold. The states were intent on retaining as much of their independence as possible. On the one hand, states wanted to protect their people from the abuses of legislative sovereignty as they had witnessed under the British Parliament, but it was clear that the Continental Congress needed some ability to govern the country to successfully conduct the war effort. The compromise that was reached was that the national government would not rule over the people directly but would only administer the actions of the states.

This principle was expressed in the second national document of the United States, the Articles of Confederation; the first was simply a temporary compact of convenience. John Dickinson presented the first draft articles to the Congress just days after the Declaration of Independence was signed in July 1776. Debate raged over the next few weeks over the question of national power. Samuel Adams and Ned Rutledge both argued for state sovereignty and against any centralized system in the new union. The other question was representation: were all the states equal in voting rights, or would they receive their share of authority based on their population or size of their territory? John Adams defended the latter position.

The matter was argued until November 1777, when Congress adopted a finalized version of the Articles. Copies were then sent to the states with anticipation that they would quickly be ratified by all of the states, with every state needed to finally implement the plan. Yet, after six months, only Virginia, New York, and New Hampshire had approved the Articles. Only in July 1778 would eight of the thirteen states sign on. Another two, North Carolina and Georgia, had approved ratification but didn't have representatives present in Philadelphia for the initial signing. Nevertheless, they were able to follow up by the end of July. Three states, New Jersey, Maryland, and Delaware, held out even longer. Maryland would be the last state to ratify the Articles in 1781, after holding out over disputed land claims. Several states had asserted their rights under their colonial charters to claim lands stretching all the way to the Mississippi River, but Maryland held out until all states agreed to forgo any claims beyond the Appalachian Mountains.

With great fanfare, the Articles of Confederation received final ratification on March 1, 1781, just months before the defeat of the British at Yorktown. The Articles hailed a "league of friendship" of "the United States of America." For almost the entire duration of the war, the Continental Congress—now the Confederation Congress—had operated under a gentleman's agreement, with the anticipation that the Articles would eventually be approved. Few expected it would take as long as it did, but now the Americans had a fully functional, constitutional government. The ratification of the Articles ended the question of representation in Congress.

Eventually, several big states, concerned with a consolidation of power in the national government, aligned with the smaller states to adopt a one-state, one-vote provision. But to prevent the smaller states from ganging up on the larger states, a majority of nine states, or two-thirds, was needed to adopt laws. States would keep almost all their power, as one of the articles made clear: "Each State retains its sovereignty, freedom and independence, and every power, jurisdiction and right, which is not by this confederation expressly delegated to the United States, in Congress assembled." Additionally, all the states would have to agree unanimously to any changes made to the Articles of Confederation, making reforms virtually impossible.

LIMITED POWER AND JURISDICTION

In the end, limited powers were given to Congress under the Articles of Confederation. They could declare war and peace, establish treaties and alliances, maintain military forces, and settle disputes among the states. The most important power withheld from Congress, however, was the right to tax citizens directly. Article 18 stated clearly that the only taxes that could be levied on the states were to support the newly established Post Office. Congress would request the funds necessary to run the government from the states, each of which would then determine how they were going to raise the revenues.

The advocates of limited government had won the day. Not only was the independence of the states preserved, but the problems of having all legislative power concentrated in a unified body, like the British Parliament, were averted. Each state was also left to regulate its own commerce and held all powers not specifically delegated to the national government. The arrangement was more than a loose association of independent nations, for the confederation of states also had a real national government to present to the rest of the world and could negotiate in good faith with other countries for their cause.

THE GREAT DEBATE

But the leaders in Congress could not anticipate the problems that the new system would create, particularly in providing financially for the Confederation government. It was far from an efficient system, as many states regularly ignored the appeals for funds. The inability for Congress to collect taxes directly and the reluctance of the states to abide by the requests resulted in the financial shortfall that made payment of the army impossible.

The result was a general dissatisfaction by the soldiers in the Continental Army that led to the riots that almost toppled the government after the war had already been won—a situation in which George Washington had to personally intervene to put them to an end. The long ordeal of forming a national government had split the country in two: into those who wanted a strong centralized government over the states and those who wanted the states to remain independent and free.

This division would grow wider during the 1780s as the American nation attempted to recover from the war's aftermath and overcome the inherent weaknesses of the Articles of Confederation. Indeed, it would constitute the first and greatest debate of American polity and life—one that continues to this day: limited and decentralized government versus expansive and centralized government.

FORGOTTEN PRESIDENTS

During the years of the War for Independence—then afterward for another six years—fifteen men served as President of the United States for the Continental and Confederation Congresses. These men led the new nation from the old colonial system to an independent country and a prominent member of the international order.

They ranged in age and experience and came from a variety of backgrounds. The first, Peyton Randolph, was the revered statesman from Virginia and Speaker of that state's pre-war House of Burgesses. Others were prominent businessmen, like John Hancock of Massachusetts, Henry Middleton, and Henry Laurens, both from South Carolina. Arthur St. Clair, born in Scotland and trained in the British army during the Seven Years' War, became an effective militia leader in the early days of the independence movement. Thomas Mifflin, a better politician than a soldier, signed the Treaty of Paris that ended the War of Independence and received George Washington's commission at the end of hostilities. Elias Boudinot of New Jersey never made a name for himself in American politics but was a crucial diplomat for his country in the early years of the war.

In all, these men served with distinction as heads of state for the infant American nation. Much like the shaky political union of the Articles of Confederation, the "forgotten Presidents" might have had very visible faults, but they served their country with distinction at a time when the cause of American independence could still be won or lost. In the troubled days to come, as the new nation grappled with the task of forming a more perfect union, America needed men of principle and men of action, for which America proved to be a fertile soil.

DIVE DEEPER: THE FORGOTTEN PRESIDENTS

Who was the first president of the United States? Ask any school child and they will readily tell you "George Washington." And of course, they would be wrong—at least technically. Washington was not inaugurated until April 30, 1789. And yet, the United States continually had functioning governments as early as September 5, 1774 and operated as a confederated nation as early as July 4, 1776. During that nearly fifteen-year interval, Congress—first the Continental Congress and then later the Confederation Congress—was always moderated by a duly elected president. As the chief executive officer of the government of the United States, the president was recognized as the head of state. Washington was thus the fifteenth—and his administration was the seventeenth—in a long line of distinguished presidents. He just happened to be the first under the current constitution. So who were the luminaries who preceded him?

PEYTON RANDOLPH OF VIRGINIA
(1723-1775)

When delegates gathered in Philadelphia for the first Continental Congress, they promptly elected the former King's Attorney of Virginia as the moderator and president of their convocation. He was a propitious choice. He was a legal prodigy—having studied at the Inner Temple in London, served as his native colony's Attorney General, and tutored many of the most able men of the South at William and Mary College, including the young Patrick Henry. His home in Williamsburg was the gathering place for Virginia's legal and political gentry, and it remains a popular attraction in the restored colonial capital. He had served as a delegate in the Virginia House of Burgesses and had been a commander under William Byrd in the colonial militia. He was a scholar of some renown, having begun a self-guided reading of the classics when he was thirteen. Despite suffering poor health, he served the Continental Congress as president twice—from September 5 to October 21, 1774 and from May 10 to May 23, 1775. He never lived to see independence, yet he was numbered among the nation's most revered founders.

HENRY MIDDLETON (1717-1784)

America's second elected president was one of the wealthiest planters in the South and the patriarch of one of the most powerful families anywhere in the nation. His public spirit was evident from an early age. He was a member of his state's Common House from 1744-1747. During the last two years he served as the Speaker. During 1755, he was the King's Commissioner of Indian Affairs. He was a member of the South Carolina Council from 1755-1770. His valor in the War with the Cherokees during 1760-1761 earned him wide recognition throughout the colonies and demonstrated his cool leadership abilities while under pressure. He was elected as a delegate to the first session of the Continental Congress, and when Peyton Randolph was forced to resign the presidency, his peers immediately turned to Middleton to complete the term. He served as the fledgling coalition's president from October 22, 1774 until Randolph was able to resume his duties briefly beginning on May 10, 1775. Afterward, he was a member of the Congressional Council of Safety and helped to establish the young nation's policy toward the encouragement and support of education. In February 1776, he resigned his political involvements in order to prepare his family and lands for what he believed was inevitable war. His son, Arthur, replaced him, however, eventually becoming a signer of the Declaration of Independence and the Articles of Confederation, an English prisoner of war, and Governor of his state.

JOHN HANCOCK (1737-1793)

The third president was a patriot, rebel leader, and merchant who signed his name into immortality in giant strokes on the Declaration of Independence on July 4, 1776. The boldness of his signature has made it live in American minds as a perfect expression of the strength and freedom—and defiance—of the individual in the face of British tyranny. As President of the Continental Congress during two widely spaced terms—the first from May 24, 1775 to October 30, 1777 and the second from November 23, 1885 to June 5, 1786—Hancock was the presiding officer when the members approved the Declaration of Independence. Because of his position, it was his official duty to sign the document first—but not necessarily as dramatically as he did. Hancock figured prominently in another historic event—the battle at Lexington. The British troops who fought there on April 10, 1775 knew Hancock and Samuel Adams were in Lexington, and they had come there to capture these rebel leaders. In fact, Hancock and Adams would have been captured if they had not been warned by Paul Revere. As early as 1768, Hancock defied the British by refusing to pay customs charges on the cargo of one of his ships. One of Boston's wealthiest merchants, he was recognized by the citizens, as well as by the British, as a rebel leader—and was elected President of the first Massachusetts Provincial Congress accordingly. After he was chosen President of the Continental Congress in 1775, Hancock became known beyond the borders of Massachusetts, and having served as colonel of the Massachusetts Governor's Guards, he hoped to be named commander of the American forces, that is, until John Adams nominated George Washington. In 1778, Hancock was commissioned Major General and took part in an unsuccessful campaign in Rhode Island. But it was as a political leader that his real distinction was earned—as the first Governor of Massachusetts, as President of Congress, and as President of the Massachusetts Constitutional Ratification Convention. He helped win ratification in Massachusetts, gaining enough popular recognition to make him a contender for the newly created Presidency of the United States, but again, he saw Washington gain the prize. Like his rival, George Washington, Hancock was a wealthy man who risked much for the cause of independence. He was the wealthiest New

Englander supporting the patriotic cause, and although he lacked the brilliance of John Adams or the capacity to inspire like Samuel Adams, he became one of the foremost leaders of the new nation—perhaps, in part, because he was willing to commit so much at such risk to the cause of freedom.

HENRY LAURENS (1724-1792)

The only American president ever to be held as a prisoner of war by a foreign power, Laurens was heralded after he was released as "the father of our country" by no less a personage than George Washington. He was of Huguenot extraction, his ancestors having come to America from France after the revocation of the Edict of Nantes made the Reformed faith illegal. Raised and educated for a life of commerce at his home in Charleston, he also had the opportunity to spend more than a year in continental travel. It was while in Europe that he began to write revolutionary pamphlets, gaining him renown as a patriot. He served as vice-president of South Carolina in 1776. He was then elected to the Continental Congress. He succeeded John Hancock as President of the newly independent but war-beleaguered United States on November 1, 1777. He served until December 9, 1778, at which time he was appointed Ambassador to the Netherlands. Unfortunately for the cause of the young nation, he was captured by an English warship during his cross-Atlantic voyage and was confined to the Tower of London until the end of the war. After the Battle of Yorktown, the American government regained his freedom in a dramatic prisoner exchange—President Laurens for Lord Cornwallis. Ever the patriot, Laurens continued to serve his nation as one of the three representatives selected to negotiate terms at the Paris Peace Conference in 1782.

JOHN JAY (1745-1829)

America's first Secretary of State, first Chief Justice of the Supreme Court, one of its first ambassadors, and author of some of the celebrated Federalist Papers, Jay was a Founding Father who, by a quirk of fate, missed signing the Declaration of Independence—at the time of the vote for independence and the signing, he had temporarily left the Continental Congress to serve in New York's revolutionary legislature. Nevertheless, he was chosen by his peers to succeed Henry Laurens as President of the United States—serving a term from December 10, 1778 to September 27, 1779. A conservative New York lawyer who was at first against the idea of independence for the colonies, in 1776, the aristocratic Jay turned into a patriot who was willing to give the next twenty-five years of his life to help establish the new nation. During those years, he won the regard of his peers as a dedicated and accomplished statesman and a man of unwavering principle. In the Continental Congress, Jay prepared addresses to the people of Canada and Great Britain. In New York, he drafted the State Constitution and served as Chief Justice during the war. He was President of the Continental Congress before he undertook the difficult assignment, as ambassador, of trying to gain support and funds from Spain. After helping Franklin, Jefferson, Adams, and Laurens complete peace negotiations in Paris in 1783, Jay returned to become the first Secretary of State, called "Secretary of Foreign Affairs" under the Articles of Confederation. He negotiated valuable commercial treaties with Russia and Morocco and dealt with the continuing controversy with Britain and Spain over the southern and western boundaries of the United States. He proposed that America and Britain establish a joint commission to arbitrate disputes that remained after the war—a proposal that, though not adopted, influenced the government's use of arbitration and diplomacy in settling later international problems. In this post, Jay felt keenly the weakness of the Articles of Confederation and was one of the first to advocate a new governmental compact. He wrote five Federalist Papers supporting the Constitution, and he was a leader in the New York ratification convention. As first Chief Justice of the Supreme Court, Jay made the historic decision that a State could be sued by a citizen from another State, which led to the Eleventh Amendment to the Constitution. On a special mission to London, he concluded the "Jay Treaty," which helped avert a renewal of hostilities with Britain but won little popular favor at home—and it is probably for this treaty that this Founding Father is best remembered.

SAMUEL HUNTINGTON (1732-1796)

An industrious youth who mastered his studies of the law without the advantage of a school, a tutor, or a master—borrowing books and snatching opportunities to read and research between odd jobs—he was one of the greatest self-made men among the Founders. He was also one of the greatest legal minds of the age—all the more remarkable for his lack of advantage as a youth. In 1764, in recognition of his obvious abilities and initiative, he was elected to the General Assembly of Connecticut. The next year, he was chosen to serve on the Executive Council. In 1774, he was appointed Associate Judge of the Superior Court and as a delegate to the Continental Congress was acknowledged to be a legal scholar of some respect. He served in Congress for five consecutive terms, during the last of which he was elected President. He served in that office from September 28, 1779 until ill health forced him to resign on July 9, 1781. He returned to his home in Connecticut, and as he recuperated, he accepted more Conciliar and Bench duties. He again took his seat in Congress in 1783 but left it to become Chief Justice of his state's Superior Court. He was elected Lieutenant Governor in 1785 and Governor in 1786. According to John Jay, he was "the most precisely trained Christian jurist ever to serve his country."

THOMAS MCKEAN (1734-1817)

During his astonishingly varied fifty-year career in public life, he held almost every possible position—from deputy county attorney to President of the United States under the Confederation. Besides signing the Declaration of Independence, he contributed significantly to the development and establishment of constitutional government in both his home state of Delaware and the nation. At the Stamp Act Congress, he proposed the voting procedure that Congress adopted, namely, that each colony, regardless of size or population, have one vote. It was a practice adopted by the Continental Congress and the Congress of the Confederation, and it was the principle of state equality manifested in the composition of the Senate. As county judge in 1765, he defied the British by ordering his court to work only with documents that did not bear the hated stamps. In June 1776, at the Continental Congress, McKean joined with Caesar Rodney to register Delaware's approval of the Declaration of Independence over the negative vote of the third Delaware delegate, George Read—permitting the document to be "The unanimous declaration of the thirteen United States." And at a special Delaware convention, he drafted the constitution for that State. McKean also helped draft—and signed—the Articles of Confederation. It was during his tenure of service as President, from July 10, 1781 to November 4, 1782, that news arrived from General Washington in October 1781 that the British had surrendered following the Battle of Yorktown. As Chief Justice of the Supreme Court of Pennsylvania, he contributed to the establishment of the legal system in that State, and, in 1787, he strongly supported the Constitution at the Pennsylvania Ratification Convention, declaring it "the best the world has yet seen." At sixty-five, after over forty years of public service, McKean resigned from his post as Chief Justice. A candidate on the Democratic-Republican ticket in 1799, McKean was elected Governor of Pennsylvania. As Governor, he followed such a strict policy of appointing only fellow Republicans to office that he became the father of the spoils system in America. He served three tempestuous terms as Governor, completing one of the longest continuous careers of public service of any of the Founding Fathers.

JOHN HANSON (1715-1783)

He was the heir of one of the greatest family traditions in the colonies and became the patriarch of a long line of American patriots—his great grandfather died at Lutzen beside the great King Gustavus Aldophus of Sweden; his grandfather was one of the founders of New Sweden along the Delaware River in Maryland;

one of his nephews was the military secretary to George Washington; another was a signer of the Declaration; still another was a signer of the Constitution; yet another was Governor of Maryland during the Revolution; and still another was a member of the first Congress; two sons were killed in action with the Continental Army; a grandson served as a member of Congress under the new Constitution; and another grandson was a Maryland Senator. Thus, even if Hanson had not served as President himself, he would have greatly contributed to the life of the nation through his ancestry and progeny. As a youngster, he began a self-guided reading of the classics and rather quickly became an acknowledged expert in the juridicalism of Anselm and the practical philosophy of Seneca—both of which were influential in the development of the political philosophy of the great leaders of the Reformation. It was based upon these legal and theological studies that the young planter—his farm, Mulberry Grove, was just across the Potomac from Mount Vernon—began to espouse the cause of the patriots. In 1775, he was elected to the Provincial Legislature of Maryland. Then, in 1777, he became a member of Congress, where he distinguished himself as a brilliant administrator. Thus, he was elected President in 1781. He served in that office from November 5, 1781 until November 3, 1782. He was the first President to serve a full term after the full ratification of the Articles of Confederation, and like so many of the Southern and New England Founders, he was strongly opposed to the Constitution when it was first discussed. He remained a confirmed anti-federalist until his untimely death.

ELIAS BOUDINOT (1741-1802)

He did not sign the Declaration, the Articles, or the Constitution. He did not serve in the Continental Army with distinction. He was not renowned for his legal mind or his political skills. He was instead a man who spent his entire career in foreign diplomacy. He earned the respect of his fellow patriots during the dangerous days following the traitorous action of Benedict Arnold. His deft handling of relations with Canada also earned him great praise. After being elected to the Congress from his home state of New Jersey, he served as the new nation's Secretary for Foreign Affairs—managing the influx of aid from France, Spain, and Holland. In 1782, he was elected to the Presidency. He served in that office from November 4, 1782 until November 2, 1783. Like so many of the other early presidents, he was a classically trained scholar of the Reformed faith and an anti-federalist in political matters. He was the father and grandfather of frontiersmen, and one of his grandchildren and namesakes eventually became a leader of the Cherokee nation in its bid for independence from the sprawling expansion of the United States.

THOMAS MIFFLIN (1744-1800)

By an ironic sort of providence, Thomas Mifflin served as George Washington's first aide-de-camp at the beginning of the Revolutionary War, and when the war was over, he was the man, as President of the United States, who accepted Washington's resignation of his commission. In the years between, Mifflin greatly served the cause of freedom—and, apparently, his own cause—while serving as the first Quartermaster General of the Continental Army. He obtained desperately needed supplies for the new army—and was suspected of making excessive profit himself. Although experienced in business and successful in obtaining supplies for the war, Mifflin preferred the front lines, and he distinguished himself in military actions on Long Island and near Philadelphia. Born and reared a Quaker, he was excluded from their meetings for his military activities. A controversial figure, Mifflin lost favor with Washington and was part of the Conway Cabal—a rather notorious plan to replace Washington with General Horatio Gates. Mifflin narrowly missed court-martial action over his handling of funds by resigning his commission in 1778. In spite of these problems and of repeated charges that he was a drunkard, Mifflin continued to be elected to positions of responsibility—President and Governor of Pennsylvania, delegate to the Constitutional Convention, and President of the Continental Congress, where he served from November 3, 1783 to November 29, 1784. Most of Mifflin's significant contributions occurred in his earlier years. In the First and Second Continental Congresses, he was firm in his stand for independence and for fighting for it, and he helped obtain both men and supplies for Washington's army in the early critical period. In 1784, as President, he signed the treaty with Great Britain, which ended the war. Although a delegate to the Constitutional Convention, he did not make a significant contribution—beyond signing the document. As Governor of Pennsylvania, although he was accused of negligence, he supported improvements of roads and reformed the State penal and judicial systems. He had gradually become sympathetic to Jefferson's principles regarding State's rights; even so, he directed the Pennsylvania militia to support the Federal tax collectors in the Whiskey Rebellion. In spite of charges of corruption, the affable Mifflin remained a popular figure. A magnetic personality and an effective speaker, he managed to hold a variety of elective offices for almost thirty years of the critical Revolutionary period.

RICHARD HENRY LEE (1732-1794)

His resolution "that these United Colonies are, and of right ought to be, free and independent States," approved by the Continental Congress July 2, 1776, was the first official act of the United Colonies that set them irrevocably on the road to independence. It was not surprising that it came from Lee's pen, for as early as 1768, he proposed the idea of committees of correspondence among the colonies. In 1774, he proposed that the colonies meet in what became the Continental Congress. From the first, his eye was on independence. A wealthy Virginia planter whose ancestors had been granted extensive lands by King Charles II, Lee disdained the traditional aristocratic role and the aristocratic view. In the House of Burgesses, he flatly denounced the practice of slavery. He saw independent America as "an asylum where the unhappy may find solace, and the persecuted repose." In 1764, when news of the proposed Stamp Act reached Virginia, Lee was a member of the committee of the House of Burgesses that drew up an address to the King, an official protest against such a tax. After the tax was established, Lee organized the citizens of his county into the Westmoreland Association, a group pledged to buy no British goods until the Stamp Act was repealed. At the First Continental Congress, Lee persuaded representatives from all the colonies to adopt this non-importation idea, leading to the formation of the Continental

Association, which was one of the first steps toward union of the colonies. Lee also proposed to the First Continental Congress that a militia be organized and armed—the year before the first shots were fired at Lexington—but this and other proposals of his were considered too radical at the time. Three days after Lee introduced his resolution, in June of 1776, Congress appointed him to the committee responsible for drafting a declaration of independence, but he was called home when his wife fell ill. His place was taken by his young protégé, Thomas Jefferson. Thus, Lee missed the chance to draft the document, though his influence greatly shaped it, and he was able to return in time to sign it. He was elected President—serving from November 30, 1784 to November 22, 1785, when he was succeeded by the second administration of John Hancock. Elected to the Constitutional Convention, Lee refused to attend, but as a member of the Congress of the Confederation, he contributed to another great document, the Northwest Ordinance, which provided for the formation of new States from the Northwest Territory. When the completed Constitution was sent to the States for ratification, Lee opposed it as anti-democratic and anti-Christian. However, as one of Virginia's first Senators, he helped assure passage of the amendments—the Bill of Rights—that he felt corrected many of the document's gravest faults. He was the great uncle of Robert E. Lee and the scion of a great family tradition.

NATHANIEL GORHAM (1738-1796)

Another self-made man, Gorham was one of the many successful Boston merchants who risked all he had for the cause of freedom. He was first elected to the Massachusetts General Court in 1771. His honesty and integrity won him acclaim, and he was thus among the first delegates chosen to serve in the Continental Congress. He remained in public service throughout the war and into the Constitutional period, though his greatest contribution was his call for a stronger central government. But even though he was an avid federalist, he did not believe that the union could—or even should—be maintained peaceably for more than a hundred years. He was convinced that eventually, in order to avoid civil or cultural war, smaller regional interests should pursue an independent course. His support of a new constitution was rooted more in pragmatism than ideology. When John Hancock was unable to complete his second term as President, Gorham was elected to succeed him—serving from June 6, 1786 to February 1, 1787. It was during this time that the Congress actually entertained the idea of asking Prince Henry—the brother of Frederick II of Prussia—and Bonnie Prince Charlie—the leader of the ill-fated Scottish Jacobite Rising and heir of the Stuart royal line—to consider the possibility of establishing a constitutional monarchy in America. It was a plan that had much to recommend it, but eventually, the advocates of republicanism held the day. During the final years of his life, Gorham was concerned with several speculative land deals, which nearly cost him his entire fortune.

ARTHUR ST. CLAIR (1734-1818)

Born and educated in Edinburgh, Scotland during the tumultuous days of the final Jacobite Rising and the Tartan Suppression, St. Clair was the only president of the United States born and bred on foreign soil. Though most of his family and friends abandoned their devastated homeland in the years following the Battle of Culloden—after which nearly a third of the land was depopulated through emigration to America—he stayed behind to learn the ways of the hated Hanoverian English in the Royal Navy. His plan was to learn of the enemy's military might in order to fight another day. During the global conflict of the Seven Years' War—generally known as the French and Indian War—he was stationed in the American theater. Afterward, he decided to settle in Pennsylvania where many of his kin had established themselves. His civic-mindedness quickly became apparent: he helped to organize both the New Jersey and the Pennsylvania militias, led the Continental Army's Canadian expedition, and was elected to Congress. His long years of training in the enemy camp were finally paying off. He was elected President in 1787—and he served from February 2 of that year until January 21 of the next. Following his term of duty in the highest office in the land, he became the first Governor of the Northwest Territory and the founder of Cincinnati. Though he briefly supported the idea of creating a constitutional monarchy under the Stuart's Bonnie Prince Charlie, he was a strident Anti-Federalist, believing that the proposed federal constitution would eventually allow for the intrusion of government into virtually every sphere and aspect of life. He even predicted that, under the vastly expanded centralized power of the state, the taxing powers of bureaucrats and other unelected officials would eventually confiscate as much as a quarter of the income of the citizens—a notion that seemed laughable at the time but that has proven to be ominously modest in light of our current governmental leviathan. St. Clair lived to see the hated English tyrants who destroyed his homeland defeated, but he despaired that his adopted home might create similar tyrannies and impose them upon itself.

CYRUS GRIFFIN (1736-1796)

Like Peyton Randolph, he was trained in London's Inner Temple to be a lawyer—and thus was counted among his nation's legal elite. Like so many other Virginians, he was an anti-federalist, though he eventually accepted the new Constitution with the promise of the Bill of Rights as a hedge against the establishment of an American monarchy, which still had a good deal of currency. The Articles of Confederation afforded such freedoms that he had become convinced that, even with the incumbent loss of liberty, some new form of government would be required. A protégé of George Washington, having worked with him on several speculative land deals in the West, he was a reluctant supporter of the Constitutional ratifying process. It was during his term in the office of the Presidency—the last before the new national compact went into effect—that ratification was formalized and finalized. He served as the nation's chief executive from January 22, 1788 until George Washington's inauguration on April 30, 1789.

CHAPTER 14: EMERGENCE OF A NATION

"The only foundation for a republic is to be laid in Religion. Without this there can be no virtue, and without virtue there can be no liberty, and liberty is the object and life of all republican governments."

BENJAMIN RUSH

With peace secured and a system of government established under the Articles of Confederation, the new American nation began the task of building a country. Free from the threat of England, Thomas Paine could write in a follow-up to his important wartime pamphlet, *The Crisis*, "The times that tried men's souls are over—and the greatest and completest revolution the world ever knew, gloriously and happily accomplished."

That kind of exuberance was, in fact, quite common. There was much for which Americans could—and should—be thankful. The threat of war was gone; the spiritual awakening seemed to be continuing apace; political and cultural toleration was now a fairly universal norm; the nation, while facing economic troubles, continued to enjoy widespread prosperity; and the state and national governments fully embraced the most far-reaching principles of liberty the world has ever seen.

There was still uncertainty, however, about the future, and there were signs that despite the ongoing effects of revival, a new moral decay was threatening to creep in. David Ramsay, son-in-law of John Witherspoon and a prominent South Carolina physician, wrote in his *History of the American Revolution*, "War never fails to injure the morals of people engaged in it [...]. On the whole, the literary, political and military talents of the citizens of the United States have been improved by the revolution, but their moral character is inferior to what it formerly was. So great is the change for the worse, that the friends of public order are fondly called upon to exert their utmost abilities, in extirpating the vicious principles and habits, which have taken deep root during the late convulsions."

Churches and clergy were hit hard by the economic troubles after the war, as ministers were paid with devalued currency, and many were forced to leave their charges in order to provide for their families. Churches burned or damaged during the conflict were not easily rebuilt, and some communities were prohibited by such circumstances from conducting regular, public worship services. The blessings of Providence that had been so evident during the conflict were all too quickly taken for granted as British soldiers began to vacate their posts.

The country was soon faced with the same problems they fought the war to settle: the extent and nature of political power, justice delayed and denied, and obstructions to the pursuit of happiness. A chief complaint of citizens and politicians alike was the inadequacy of the Articles of Confederation. The division grew wider between those wanting small, limited government and those advocating a strong, centralized government. As the 1780s progressed, America would have to revisit these struggles and resolve them anew.

RENEWED RELATIONS WITH ENGLAND

Even before the end of the war, Congress had charged five commissioners, Ben Franklin, John Adams, Thomas Jefferson, John Jay, and Henry Laurens, to travel to Paris in order to finalize a peace treaty with Great Britain. Jefferson never went, and Laurens was captured and imprisoned in the Tower of London by the British for over a year before his release. That left Franklin, Adams, and Jay to finish the work. The most important aspect in their negotiations was to secure England's acknowledgment of independence. They also had to be mindful of the other countries, such as France, Spain, and the Netherlands, who wanted to ensure that the treaty would benefit their positions as well. Congress specifically instructed the commissioners to consider France's interests because of their involvement in securing the defeat of the British at Yorktown.

John Jay's diplomatic mission to Spain had been a complete failure, and he considered Spain an enemy to America now that the war had ended. The Spanish were already secretly negotiating with the British to regain the island of Gibraltar, and they wanted to expand their American holdings to include the disputed territory east of the Mississippi River. England made it clear that they wanted to hold onto Florida. In the end, because Ben Franklin was also wary of French intentions in America, the three negotiators decided to ignore their instructions from Congress and deal directly with Lord Shelburne, Secretary of State for Foreign Affairs, for a peace treaty between America and England.

Franklin drafted a proposal and submitted it to the British negotiators for their consideration. The demand for recognition of independence was a given, but the boundaries of the colonies, the redrawing of the Canadian border further north, and the secured rights of American fishermen to sail in the waters off Newfoundland and Nova Scotia were considered to be essential points for the American position as well. The British wanted to be sure the Loyalists still in America were protected from retribution and that American merchants repaid their debts to British bankers. Both sides agreed that the Spanish should be kept out of the lands east of the Mississippi.

Without the intervention of the other countries, the two sides quickly reached an initial agreement. Congress approved the Treaty of Paris and the English and American negotiators gathered on September 3, 1783 to put an official end to the War of Independence and to reestablish relations between the two countries. American independence was granted, and the British agreed to withdraw all troops from the United States at once. The boundaries of Canada were moved north of the Great Lakes, back to their position before the Quebec Act of 1774, and the United States obtained all the territory east of the Mississippi, effectively locking out the Spanish, while still allowing the British free navigation rights along the river. Fishing rights off the Canadian coast were guaranteed for New England fishermen, and assurances were given that Loyalists would have their property returned and would not suffer any further losses. Creditors on both sides would be paid in full in sterling money, not with the devalued paper currency. It was only after negotiations were concluded that the French and Spanish were informed of the deal.

The Treaty of Paris was a diplomatic success for America. George Washington hailed the agreement and noted the beneficial position that the treaty created for the country: "The citizens of America, places in the most enviable condition, as the sole lords and proprietors of a vast tract of continent, comprehending all the various soils and climates of the world, and abounding with all the necessaries and conveniences of life, are now, by the late satisfactory pacification, acknowledged to be possessed of absolute freedom and independence."

THE ARTICLES' CROWNING ACHIEVEMENT

Congress quickly began to discuss what to do with the new territories acquired under the peace treaty. Prior to the outbreak of war, Virginia claimed most of the land west of the Appalachians. When she first ceded this land to the Continental Congress, it was with so many restrictions that Congress at first rejected the offer. In 1784, however, Virginia turned over the land with no strings attached, and Congress accepted it.

Immediately, Congress began to draw up plans for settling this Northwest Territory. Thomas Jefferson was given the responsibility of writing up these plans. He decided to carve up the territory into ten equal districts. When a district had twenty thousand settlers it could hold a convention, write up its constitution, and send a delegate to Congress. As soon as its population was equal to that of the smallest state, the district could be admitted to the union as an equal of the original thirteen. Jefferson's Land

Ordinance of 1784 called for the prohibition of slavery in the entire territory, though Congress decided to ignore this provision.

Jefferson's plan of settlement was extraordinary. Instead of creating colonies dependent upon a "mother country" east of the mountains, the Americans had arranged for new settlements that would eventually become equal to older ones. No other such arrangement existed in the world at that time. While Congress adopted the Land Ordinance of 1784, it was never actually put into effect.

The following year, Congress passed the Land Ordinance of 1785, which divided up the Northwest Territory into townships and ranges. Most of New England and the Mid-Atlantic states had been settled according to an organized arrangement, whereas the settlements in the Southern states had developed independently and were scattered across the map. To avoid this problem, the township system was used, particularly since this made the land easier to sell and to verify claims. This system for laying out the Northwest Territory worked so well that it became the basis for surveying and selling most new lands which the United States would eventually acquire across the entire continent.

On July 13, 1787, while the Constitutional Convention was meeting in Philadelphia, the Continental Congress passed one of its last, and probably its most important, statute: the Northwest Ordinance of 1787. This act withdrew the immediate self-government allowed by Jefferson's 1784 ordinance, temporarily treating the Northwest Territory as part of a colonial empire. Congress was empowered to appoint a governor, secretary, and three judges to control the territory. As soon as the territory contained five thousand free, adult males, the residents could then elect their own general assembly and pass their own laws, though the appointed governor had the power to veto any legislation.

The Ordinance stipulated that at least three, but no more than five, new states could be formed from the Northwest Territory. Whenever sixty thousand free inhabitants resided in any of the states, they could draw up their own constitution and apply for admission to the Union. The Ordinance kept Jefferson's original proposal that new states be admitted as equals, revived Jefferson's ban on slavery throughout the territory, and provided a bill of rights assuring settlers they retained the freedoms they had before in the original thirteen states. Though originally intended to apply only to the Northwest Territory, the Northwest Ordinance established the pattern by which nearly every other state since that time has been admitted to the Union.

WEAKNESSES OF THE CONFEDERATION

With the war over, there seemed to be less reason for the newly independent states to work together. The second paragraph of the Articles of Confederation had made it clear that each one was jealous of its own rights: "Each State retains its sovereignty, freedom, and independence, and every power, jurisdiction, and right, which is not by this Confederation expressly delegated to the United States in Congress assembled."

Because the Founding Fathers had feared the tyranny that would result from an overly strong central government, the Confederation had expressly delegated to the United States very few powers, leaving it weak and often helpless in the face of danger. For example, Congress could not control trade and had no power to tax. It could not meet its obligation to pay off war debts.

Congress could only ask the states for money and could not force them to pay. The articles created no strong executive officer, no national court system, and no army or navy. Furthermore, most legislation had to have the unanimous approval of all thirteen states. A tiny state like Rhode Island could—and did—veto crucial legislation passed by the other twelve.

There were structural problems with both the state constitutions and the articles that needed attention. While most states tried to incorporate a separation of powers between the executive, legislative, and judicial branches of government, these divisions frequently were nothing more than paper fictions. One frequent conflict seen in the states was the legislative branch regularly overruling or altering the judgments of the judiciary. One notable example was New Hampshire, which, despite a clear statement of separation of powers in its 1784 constitution, regularly intervened in court cases and annulled verdicts. Justice rendered in courts could be easily reversed for those with influential connections in the legislature. Thus, no independent judiciary could be established that could render final verdicts in controversies.

The state legislatures also rarely had defined powers. States passed laws that deprived masses of people of their property rights by a simple majority in the legislature and that, not unlike the powers exerted by the British Parliament that provoked the War of Independence, should have required constitutional amendment. The liberties that many thought secure with the defeat of the English quickly fell subject to petty legislative tyrants in their home states.

Furthermore, the Confederation Congress was powerless to stop these abuses. After 1783, the Congress grew more ineffective as few representatives came to sessions and not enough members were present to legitimately conduct business. Even if they had enough members to constitute a quorum, the Congress had few powers to exercise. The body was wholly a creature of the states and completely subject to the whims of the state legislatures.

The British, the French, and the Spanish looked with contempt at this weak, defenseless, new nation. Why, the British wondered, should they keep all the terms of the Treaty of Paris? Being without an army or a navy, the United States was so feeble that it could do nothing about any violation. The Europeans considered the possibility of waiting a few years and then re-establishing themselves in the areas they formerly held in America. To make matters worse, the Muslim states of North Africa stopped American ships and forced them to pay tribute in order to be allowed to sail in the Mediterranean.

Overseas enemies were not the only ones to threaten the newly freed colonists. States got into trade wars by putting import taxes on goods coming in from other states. This only resulted in higher prices for everyone. New York and New Hampshire farmers shot at each other over disputed land. Virginia and Maryland fishermen quarreled over fishing rights and the boundary between their states. Many who had fought so hard and sacrificed and suffered so much for American independence wondered whether it had all been in vain.

TIME FOR ACTION

Washington wrote a circular letter to state governors in which he said, "There should be lodged somewhere a supreme power to regulate the general concerns of the Confederated Republic, without which this Union cannot be of long duration." As matters worsened, he gloomily wrote, "I predict the worst consequences for a half-starved limping government, always moving on crutches, and tottering at every step."

When the quarrel between Maryland and Virginia worsened to the point where some feared a shooting war, Washington personally intervened by inviting representatives of the two states to meet as guests in his home to discuss the issue. The success of the Mount Vernon Conference in 1785 convinced the Virginia delegates that a similar meeting of representatives of all the states the following year would be helpful. The resulting Annapolis Convention, which met in September of 1786, proved disappointing, as only five states responded by sending a dozen delegates. These twelve men, led by Alexander Hamilton, decided to call for a meeting the following summer in Philadelphia, comprised of representatives from all the states, in order to "take into consideration the situation of the United States [...]."

It was not until February of 1787 that the Confederation Congress in Philadelphia got around to officially calling for a convention. When they did, they said that it would be "for the sole purpose of revising the Articles of Confederation [...]." An electrifying event occurred in Massachusetts between August 1786 and February 1787, which helped generate excitement for the Philadelphia meeting and the revolutionary changes that it would produce.

DEBTS, DUTIES, AND DANIEL SHAYS

As soon as the war had ended, ships came from all over the world and flooded the markets with all sorts of goods. Americans eagerly purchased them with both cash and credit. Cash sales drained much gold and silver from the country, while credit sales left many people in debt to the merchants who imported foreign goods.

To make matters worse, the years from 1784 to 1787 were marked by an economic depression. This is a common occurrence following a war. Many goods produced for the military were no longer needed, which meant that many people producing them no longer had jobs. At the same time, returning soldiers were looking for work, so unemployment ran high. In the midst of this, the Confederation government canceled hundreds of millions of dollars of debt it owed to the Americans who had served the country in its struggle for independence. Former Revolutionary soldiers who had been paid in paper money found that this "money" was now worthless. Some who needed ready cash found speculators who bought their worthless Continental currency for a few cents for every dollar of face value.

The states also had huge debts from the war, and some of them added to their debts by taking over some of the debts the Confederation government owed to their citizens. But to pay off these debts, state governments had to raise taxes. The burden of these new taxes fell most heavily on farmers, particularly small farmers living far away from the center of political power in their state capitals.

While the Continental Army had often been paid in paper money, which only had value if people chose to honor it as money, many state governments passed laws requiring that creditors—people to whom debtors owed money—and the state tax collectors be paid off in specie—hard money such as gold or silver. Very little specie was still in circulation. When debtors were unable to pay off their creditors or the tax collectors, their property was seized and sold at sheriff's auction.

Many New England farmers who had lost their farms or were about to lose them rioted. In western Massachusetts, they found a former military captain named Daniel Shays to lead them. Shays organized and drilled his followers. He and his followers then demanded that the state cut back taxes, temporarily cancel the payment of debts, abolish the use of imprisonment for debt, remove the state capital from Boston to the interior, and print large quantities of paper money. Paper money would cause inflation—technically, an increase in the supply of money rather than simply a rise in prices—and make it easier for debtors to pay their debts using money that was cheaper and easier to obtain.

During the summer of 1786, armed bands of Shaysites went around breaking up sheriffs' sales of property and disrupting court sittings that dealt with people in debt. Boston legislators like Samuel Adams denounced Shays and his men as rebels and traitors.

Late in 1786, the Shaysites marched to Springfield, Massachusetts, to get weapons from the arsenal there. In January, some four thousand militiamen, led by General Benjamin Lincoln, confronted the rebels, killed several, captured many more, and sent the rest fleeing into the hills in a blinding snowstorm. Shays and his chief aids were captured and sentenced to death, but they were soon pardoned. The state granted some tax relief and allowed for the postponement of some debts.

The greatest consequence of Shays' Rebellion, though, was the fear of rebellion that swept the country. Shays and his followers had demonstrated how helpless the Confederation government was to come to the aid of a state faced with a serious rebellion.

The pressing problems did not escape the notice of some of the prominent American leaders, including Thomas Jefferson and John Adams. Jefferson noted the encroachment of state legislatures upon the other two branches in his *Notes of Virginia*, and he complained that the concentration of power in the hands of legislators was "precisely the definition of despotic powers." John Adams advocated extensive state legislative reforms in his *Defense of the Constitutions*, but he emphasized that the reforms needed to be completed on the local level, not on a national scale. Unfortunately, Adams and Jefferson were both out of the country, in Holland and France respectively, and were not able to participate in the Philadelphia Convention.

John Jay had also proposed a set of resolutions, while serving as Secretary of Foreign Affairs in October 1786, which advocated legislative and judicial reforms in the states. Congress promptly passed these resolutions and forwarded them to the states for their approval. But as delegates arrived in Philadelphia during the summer of 1787 with the charge to amend the Articles to make them more effective, many there had determined to do something far more drastic.

DIVE DEEPER: NATIONALISM

The whole idea of nationality, and even the mood of nationalistic sentiment that gave rise to that idea, is a modern innovation in the affairs of men. It is an idea that, until just a short time ago, was utterly remote from the experience of Western civilization. Even the vocabulary of nationalism is of a very recent vintage: it was not until well into the nineteenth century that the institutional phrases we take for granted today—like "state," "polity," "federal," "government," or even "nation"—came into common usage. As short a time ago as the founding of the American republic, those engaging in political discourse preferred to speak of "the commonwealth," "the people," "the confederation," "the common land," "the public," "the community," or "the cooperative welfare" in order to avoid the centralizing and unitary implications of "nationhood." The New English Dictionary underscored that distinction as late as 1908 when it stated that the old meaning of "nationality" envisaged "little more than an ethnic unit" but that a wholly new meaning had begun to emerge that stressed the notion of "political unity and independence."

At virtually no time in the past—but especially at no time during the age of Christendom—did men identify themselves in terms of a particular nation-state. Instead, they saw themselves as members of a family or a community—or, even more likely, of a faith. Jurisdictions and boundaries were set according to these relational and covenantal loyalties rather than by governmental edicts. Thus, patriotism was interpersonal rather than institutional.

Most Americans generally did not see themselves as citizens of the United States. Their identity was not defined by a temporal state, but an eternal estate. Their sense of purpose was rooted in who they were rather than where they were from or what they did. As difficult as it may be for us to comprehend, this is the most significant clue to understanding their motivations, their ideals, their aspirations, and, ultimately, their actions. They saw themselves first and foremost as co-heirs of a united vision of liberty rather than subjects of a particular magistratal jurisdiction.

Though the systemic and ideological notions of Enlightenment nationalism had gained more and more favor with the western world's political elites since the time of the French Revolution, it was still remote enough from the day-to-day existence of Americans to be practically unnoticed.

That is why any map of the world from those days is so mind-bogglingly indecipherable to us—it portrays a forgotten philosophy as well as a forgotten geography. There did not yet exist such nation-states as Germany, Italy, or Belgium. And the United States were plural sovereignties confederated together not a singular federal union. Though it seems to be a very strange notion to us today, it is nevertheless an essential notion to understand if we are to ever grasp the Founders' vision of Federalism.

CHAPTER 15: A MORE PERFECT UNION

"In questions of power, then, let no more be heard of confidence in man, but bind him down from mischief by the chains of the Constitution."

THOMAS JEFFERSON

On May 25, 1787, fifty-five delegates chosen by the legislatures of twelve states assembled in Independence Hall in Philadelphia to "amend" the Articles of Confederation. Patrick Henry of Virginia, like many others, had doubts about the true purpose of the convention. He refused to come, saying, "I smell a rat." Only Rhode Island, called "Rogue Island" by some for their obstructions to changes of the Articles and their isolationist political mood, refused to send any representatives whatsoever.

The delegates included some of the most able and respected men in America at the time. Dr. Benjamin Franklin, at eighty-one, was the oldest delegate. Widely esteemed, he used his ability to bring about compromise at tense moments. James Madison would contribute his great learning from a careful study he had made of hundreds of written constitutions from republics past and present. Also in attendance was the most respected man of the day, George Washington, whose leadership had almost single-handedly held together a ragtag army in the face of overwhelming odds. His integrity was unquestioned; everyone there trusted him completely. They elected Washington to be their chairman, a brilliant move that they hoped might ensure their success.

At the start, the delegates decided that all sessions would meet in secret until they had finished their work. This measure would promote free discussion without fear of public pressure and keep rumors at a minimum. With the operating details agreed upon, the Convention quickly took to the business at hand.

BIG STATES, BIG GOVERNMENT

The first proposal made to the Philadelphia Convention was the Virginia Plan or the Large State Plan, presented by Edmund Randolph but probably written with the assistance of James Madison. It called for scrapping the Articles completely and replacing it with "a strong *consolidated* government." Its centerpiece was a bicameral legislature with both houses having representation based on population. This legislature would select both the executive and judiciary, could call out troops to coerce "rebellious" states, and could veto any state law that was not in agreement with the Constitution. The states with smaller populations were alarmed, fearing that this plan would result in their destruction. They knew their history. All too often small countries surrounded by large countries were gobbled up. What was the difference, they wondered, in being taken over by ballots instead of bullets? They would still lose their independence and identity.

SMALL STATES, SMALL GOVERNMENT

For two weeks the delegates debated the Virginia plan. Then, on June 15, William Paterson of New Jersey reminded the convention that it had been called solely to amend the Articles. To that end, he proposed an alternative that favored the smaller states. It became known as the New Jersey Plan or Small State Plan. It granted Congress the additional powers of levying taxes and regulating commerce but kept the unicameral legislature of the Articles, in which voting was by state, with each state having equal representation. The larger states protested that their greater population entitled them to more representation. The convention quickly rejected the New Jersey Plan, but many delegates realized that unless they made concessions to the smaller states on the issue of representation, the small states would walk out. For a while, neither side would budge from its position.

It began to seem to many delegates that the combination of the sweltering summer heat with the hot tempers of two sides unwilling to compromise might cause everyone just to give up and go home. During these critical days, on a hot July morning, Benjamin Franklin asked to be recognized. He reminded the delegates that God governed the affairs of men and suggested that He be consulted in their deliberations.

COMPROMISE

Not long after Franklin's speech, a breakthrough occurred. Delegate Roger Sherman of Connecticut offered a compromise, which became known as the Connecticut Compromise or Great Compromise. There would be a two-house legislative branch for the new government known as the United States Congress. One house of Congress, the House of Representatives, would base representation upon population and would favor the states with the largest populations. This house would be most responsive to the voters since the people would directly elect its members every two years. In the other house, the Senate, each state would be equal. Two Senators from each state would be chosen by the state legislatures to serve six-year terms.

The Great Compromise included within it another compromise based on a growing sectional tension. Southern slaveholders had wanted all their slaves counted for purposes of representation but not counted for taxation. Northerners, on the other hand, wanted all the slaves counted for taxes but none counted for representation. The convention decided to make each slave count as three fifths of a person for purposes of both taxation and representation.

Differences between North and South led to yet another major compromise. The Southern states knew that Northern states could easily outvote them in Congress and feared that they would enact bills designed to promote their manufacturing and shipping interests at the expense of Southern states. Southern states demanded that a two-thirds majority be required to enact all legislation relating to commerce and foreign trade. The South also feared that Northern states would place an export tax on the crops that were the mainstay of its economy: tobacco, rice, cotton. Finally, the South feared that Congress might suddenly cut off its supply of African slaves. The resulting compromise gave the North a very important victory by stating that only a simple majority vote in Congress would be required to pass laws regulating commerce. In exchange for this concession, the South received a clause in the Constitution that prohibited export taxes, another clause which prohibited the ending of the slave trade for at least twenty years, a third which required all states to return fugitive slaves, and a provision requiring a two-thirds majority in the Senate to ratify all treaties, many of which were expected to deal with foreign commerce.

REINING IN THE RULER

Another hot debate concerned the nature of the office of President. Many delegates feared that tyranny would be the greatest threat to the new republic and vigorously argued for a weak chief executive officer. Others, like James Madison and Alexander Hamilton, who favored a strong central government, argued for a powerful Presidency. They prevailed, but only because the delegates found a way to keep a powerful President from abusing his authority. They restrained his power with a system of Constitutional checks and balances. For example, while the President was commander-in-chief of the armed forces, only Congress had the power to declare war and raise the funds to fight it. Though the President could veto bills passed by Congress, a two-thirds vote of Congress could override his veto. The President could make appointments to high office, but he could do so only with the "advice and consent" of the Senate. Although he could negotiate treaties, they went into effect only after two-thirds of the Senate approved them. These checks on the power of the Presidency helped win over some delegates who feared giving him so much power, but there was one argument that was even more persuasive. Every delegate knew who the first President would be, and each one had the utmost confidence that this President would never abuse his power. Trust in the character of George Washington did the most to sway doubting delegates about granting significant powers to the President.

Then came the question of how to elect the President. The Virginia Plan had called for the President to be chosen by Congress for a single seven-year term. Other delegates argued that the people should elect him. In the end, the convention decided to create the Electoral College. Each state would choose electors equal in number to the total of their Senators and Representatives. The candidate who received a majority of the votes cast by the electors would become President for four years. If no one received a majority, the House of Representatives would choose the President from the top five candidates. The runner-up would become Vice-President.

Convention delegates had expected that all elections following that of Washington would end up in the House, which would still ensure the indirect election of the President. What the delegates did not foresee was the development of political parties. In most elections since Washington's, only two parties have each fielded a single candidate, meaning that one or the other was certain to receive a majority of the votes, keeping the election from going into the House. Third or fourth candidates have rarely gained enough votes to prevent someone from receiving a majority of the electoral votes.

The convention delegates had actually written very little that was original. The various officers of government, their powers and duties, and the limitations to their powers were patterned after those in state government. Much of the Constitution was borrowed from colonial or state constitutions or even from legislation passed under the Articles of Confederation. When there was uncertainty or controversy, the Constitution was left vague. Later generations were expected to work out the details. The overriding goal of the convention was to establish a workable government. The delegates knew the Constitution, as a creation of man, was not perfect, so they wrote into it a method by which it could be changed or amended if necessary.

TO THE STATES

On Monday, September 17, 1787, the Constitutional Convention officially ended. On that day, the Convention sent signed copies of the Constitution to the Confederation Congress to pass on to the state legislatures. Delegates anticipated tough battles in the states over whether the Constitution ought to be ratified.

Surprisingly, there was much that proponents and opponents of the Constitution agreed upon. First was the general mistrust of men to use power well and wisely. Power, whether in a monarchy or a republic, tended to corrupt whoever wielded it, and checks and balances between institutions were needed to obstruct the consolidation of power. They also tended to agree that direct democracy could easily be subverted through manipulation of the masses. Thus, all accepted the idea of representative government. And both sides stressed the necessity of ensuring that the representatives that governed were virtuous men. The difficulty was how to guarantee that they would be.

CHOOSING SIDES

Almost immediately, state legislatures began to be divided between those for or against the proposed constitution. In the debates that followed over the next few months, the disagreements between the Federalists, who supported ratification, and Anti-Federalists, who opposed it, would attract the most attention. The primary question that both parties had to address was how to make the national government work.

The Federalists believed that the problem of the Articles was that not enough power had been given to Confederation Congress to compel the states to abide by its requests for funds and too much power was held by the state legislatures, who passed measures to interfere with interstate commerce and printed millions in inflated currency. Their solution was to broaden the scope of the national government by giving it the power to tax and to regulate commerce and by prohibiting states from interfering in international affairs.

James Madison, one of the leading Federalists, believed that expanding the control of the national government over a large area would reduce the regional conflicts and that granting only specific, or enumerated, powers to the new government would preserve the independence of the states. Madison, along with two friends, Alexander Hamilton and John Jay, authored a series of newspaper articles in support of the plan, called *The Federalist Papers*, which are still considered to be among the greatest works of political thought in history. They felt that a strong central government with separation of powers would curb the tendency towards tyranny and at last create an effective national government.

The Anti-Federalists countered that because the government would be so large, it would not be very representative. The House of Representatives would initially only have sixty-five members to represent the whole of America. They also expressed concern that republican forms of government had historically been effective only in governing limited areas, not a whole nation stretched out along the coast of a continent and all the way to the Mississippi. The checks and balances incorporated into the new government were also suspect. The Anti-Federalists believed that there were not enough checks and that, despite the attempts to achieve a separation of powers between the three branches of government, there were still significant overlaps of power and jurisdiction that could easily lead to tyranny. It was hard to distinguish between the new Congress and the British Parliament, which claimed absolute sovereignty.

Some expressed concern that the government could quickly become "full of pagans." While no one doubted the sincerity or intentions of any of the present leadership in America, the clause prohibiting religious oaths, which were incorporated into almost every state constitution, eliminated one of the assurances that members of the government would be virtuous and adhere to the Christian religion. The constitutional debates also split many denominations, including the Presbyterians, but the Baptists in the South were overwhelming opposed to it.

Finally, nothing in the proposed Constitution enumerated the common law rights that the Americans had fought England to preserve. There was no mention regarding freedom of religion or freedom of the press, both of which were hotly contested before and during the War for Independence. While the Constitution granted the right of *habeas corpus* and a trial by jury in criminal cases, there was no specification as to how juries would be selected, where trials could be conducted, whether the accused could be represented by an attorney, or even, prohibitions against cruel and unusual punishment. There were no safeguards for these important liberties to be found in the Constitution, and Anti-Federalists made a good deal of political hay by publicizing the unpopular comments made by Alexander Hamilton—who had defended the absence of a bill of rights in the Constitution, arguing that enumerating such rights might actually be dangerous.

Many thoughtful and patriotic Americans, like Patrick Henry, opposed the Constitution because they feared that the states would lose power and that Americans would lose their liberties. Henry distrusted the office of the President, which he thought "squints toward monarchy." It would take very little, he thought, for the President to make himself into an American king. Moreover, he feared the potential for the abuse of power that would come as the result of substituting taxation for the old system of making requisitions to the states.

Other state leaders felt that the Articles could be amended to remedy their defects. New York's Governor George Clinton also made a valid point when he noted that the nation's economy was improving and that it seemed senseless to change to a new and untried government when the old one was beginning to work quite well.

With tensions high, many of the states moved ahead with the debate. On December 7, 1787, Delaware became the first state to ratify the Constitution, voting unanimously in favor of the new government. Other smaller states quickly followed. The battle over ratification in Pennsylvania was more contentious, and the final vote was split 46-23 in favor of the Constitution. In February, Massachusetts ratified, but only after a hard-fought battle and a close vote of 187-168. New Hampshire required two conventions to ratify, and even then, it passed by a very narrow margin on June 21, 1788. New Hampshire was the ninth state in favor of ratification, which represented the two-thirds required by the Constitution for it to go into effect. The Constitution was now official, and preparations were made to install the new government.

TIPPING THE BALANCE

Yet four states remained out of the union. Two of them, New York and Virginia, were among the largest and most important states. Their ratification was essential if the new union was to succeed. In Virginia, Patrick Henry and George Mason had led the fight for the Anti-Federalists and seemed on the verge of victory until Edmund Randolph, who had refused to sign the Constitution during the Convention, suddenly changed his mind. The influence of George Washington no doubt swayed many Virginians. But the deciding factor seemed to be the promise from James Madison, the leading Federalist, that the first amendments to the Constitution would be a bill of rights. Another prominent member of the Federalist faction, John Marshall, would play an important role in the shaping of the new government. The ratification vote was a close 89-79, and Virginia stated explicitly that, while she voluntarily entered into the new Federal union, she had the right to leave this union if it was in her best interests.

It was in New York that *The Federalist Papers* had their largest impact, as two of their authors, Alexander Hamilton and John

Jay, were part of the state's convention. Even so, they did little to sway New Yorkers. It was the change of heart of a leading Antifederalist that secured ratification, and then, only by three votes—30-27. North Carolina delayed their vote until November 1789, and Rhode Island became the last state to ratify on May 29, 1790.

While North Carolina and Rhode Island continued to hold out, a new Congress, now operating under the terms of the Constitution, was convened in New York and a presidential election was held in January 1789. There was little surprise at the results: the Electoral College chose George Washington as the next president, and John Adams, who had placed second, became Vice President.

FIRST IN WAR, FIRST IN PEACE

Washington was at his home, Mount Vernon, in Virginia when he received the news that he was to succeed Cyrus Griffin—an old and dear friend in the emerging Virginia political aristocracy that also included Jefferson, Madison, and Monroe—as the next president. Washington immediately set off for New York for the inauguration, and he was greeted all along his path by militia escorts and crowds of well-wishers. More than 20,000 people lined the route as he approached Philadelphia, where he enjoyed festivities arranged for him by the leading members of the city, including a massive fireworks display. When he reached New York, he was greeted by the Governor and many other public officials. A house had been prepared for his arrival, and April 30, 1789 was set as the date for him to take the oath of office.

On that day, all the clergy in New York City had called on their congregations to participate in worship services to pray for the new President and the people of the United States. At noon, Washington and John Adams left for Federal Hall, accompanied by a large contingent of troops. More than 10,000 spectators gathered for the event. In the presence of former president Griffin, George Washington took the oath of office administered by R.R. Livingston, the Chancellor of the State of New York, with his left hand on a Bible, saying: "I do solemnly swear that I will faithfully execute the office of President of the United States, and will, to the best of my ability, preserve, protect, and defend the constitution of the United States."

America now had a new president. The members of Congress then assembled in the Senate chamber, where Washington delivered an inaugural address, thanking the country and the Congress for their veneration and love and promising to recognize his weakness as he administered his office as President. Concluding his speech, he invoked the assistance of God, "so His Divine blessing may be equally conspicuous in the enlarged views, the temperate consultations, and the wise measures, on which the success of this government must depend." Washington, Adams, and Congress then left to attend a worship service to acknowledge their commitment to seek God's favor in governing America.

A NEW AMERICAN ERA

Most Americans greeted the change from one constitution to another with renewed optimism in the great experiment of liberty that they had begun just a few years earlier. A few months after Washington's inauguration, ten new amendments to the new compact—a Bill of Rights—were submitted to Congress and the states for approval, which assured those who still had concerns about having their freedoms taken away or subverted. It seemed that the trials of the past were over. But deep divisions remained. The battle over constitutional ratification had created factions within the states, which represented conflicting views of how to govern properly and effectively. These lines would be visible for many years to come. The Constitution had delayed any consideration of the slavery question for another twenty years, leaving an open sore to fester with political and social infection.

But even those who had argued most strenuously against ratifying the Constitution hoped for a new beginning. Patrick Henry, who was still the leading statesman in Virginia, was willing to give the Constitution a chance, although he declined several offices in the new government offered by Washington, including Chief Justice of the Supreme Court.

The members of the new government, now installed, put their hands to the plow to begin to right the problems that had grown worse in the previous years. There were economic obstacles to overcome and political hostilities to mend. Social unrest was still a problem and international threats still loomed on American shores and on the open seas. There can be little doubt that the nation had gone through many difficulties during the years from the Treaty of Paris in 1783 to Washington's inauguration in 1789, but Americans were nonetheless looking ahead. Everyone realized there was still much work to be done to "form a more perfect Union."

Ben Franklin had witnessed first-hand the momentous events that had taken place in his time. He had a hand in drafting the

Declaration of Independence, was the chief negotiator for the Treaty of Paris that ended the war, and had put his signature on the new Constitution, which he believed had laid a solid foundation for the future. Franklin spoke for many Americans about this new era of optimism and good hopes for the days ahead when he addressed the Constitutional Convention on the last day of its sitting. He said that the United States, now free from English rule and in control of its own destiny under a new government, had arrived at a new era. America, the great experiment of liberty, was "a rising, and not a setting sun."

DIVE DEEPER: FEDERALISM

No other instrument of government—ancient or modern—produced such stability, offered such freedom, enjoyed such prosperity, or conveyed such hope as the American Constitution. Amazingly, during more than two centuries of social, cultural, political, and technological revolution throughout the entire world, this document has endured, fundamentally unchanged.

All the other European social contracts, manifestos, national charters, and constitutions of the eighteenth century have long since been consigned to the dust bin of history. The lofty ambitions ensconced in the constitutions of Latin America, drawn up in the halcyon days of their newfound independence, have all vanished. All the nationalist declarations, drawn up in the heady days following the First World War, are likewise gone. Those constitutions promulgated at the end of the Second World War have hardly fared better. And there is little doubt that the same fate yet awaits the emerging democracies that have begun dotting the maps of Europe, Asia, and Africa following the collapse of Communism.

Through it all, the American Constitution has flourished. It is a creed that has withstood every test.

Drawing on a great wealth of sage knowledge and practical experience, the Founding Fathers codified in their national charter a whole host of carefully wrought provisions, provisions designed to preserve the freedoms and liberties of the people. They designed the government with a series of interlocking checks and balances—not only were the executive, legislative, and judicial branches given spheres of authority over which the others could not interfere, but localities, regions, states, and even individuals were also afforded certain hedges against the imposition of tyranny. Powers were carefully separated. Authorities were circumspectly delineated. Rights were vigilantly secured.

Rather than yield to the inherent weaknesses of pure democracy, absolute monarchy, elitist oligarchy, radical republicanism, or haughty aristocracy, the Founders created the Constitution as a bastion of a kind of mixed government known as Federalism. It was to be a confederation of accountable spheres and covenantal sovereignties. It provided the nation with a government of laws, not rulers. It established a legacy of limited government, as Jefferson asserted, "laced up straitly within enumerated powers."

History has proven the brilliance of the plan. Hardly the fruit of an antiquarian system meant for an agrarian people, the Constitution's genius is that it is, as President Calvin Coolidge once asserted, "grounded upon a firm foundation of enduring principles, applicable to any society for any time." It is a creed. It is the very quintessence of American exceptionalism.

The essential philosophical and structural framework within which the Founding Fathers constructed their innovative scheme of national checks and balances, separation of powers, and mixed government was state confederation—or federalism. The principle of federalism allows distinctive and individual communities to join together for a greater good without losing their essential distinctiveness and individuality. Instead of the states becoming a part of some larger amorphous union, under federalism, they are able to unite in a symbiotic fashion so that the sum of their parts is greater than that of the whole. A federal relationship is a kind of compact or covenant that allows states to bind themselves together substantially without entirely subsuming their sundry identities. The federal nature of the American Constitutional covenant enables the nation to function as a republic—thus specifically avoiding the dangers of a pure democracy. Republics exercise governmental authority through mediating representatives under the rule of law. Pure democracies, on the other hand, exercise governmental authority through the imposition of the will of the majority without regard for the concerns of any minority—thus allowing law to be subject to the whims, fashions, and fancies of men. The Founders designed the federal system of the United States so that the nation could be, as John Adams described it, a "government of law, not of men."

The Founders thus expressly and explicitly rejected the idea of a pure democracy, because, as James Madison declared, "democracies have ever been spectacles of turbulence and contention; have ever been found incompatible with personal security, or the rights of property; and have in general been as short in their lives, as they have been violent in their deaths." The rule of the majority does not always respect the rule of law and is as turbulent as the caprices of political correctness. Indeed, history has proven all too often that democracy is particularly susceptible to the urges and impulses of mobocracy.

Federalism balances the vertical and horizontal aspects of a covenant. Vertically, Americans are one people under the rule of common law. Horizontally, though, Americans are differentiated into a number of distinctive communities—sovereign states—protected from the possible intrusions of the national government or from a majority of the other communities. As educator Paul Jehle has argued, "The nature of federalism is seen in the balanced structure of the states and the people throughout the Constitution. Both the national government and State governments are sovereign in their respective spheres. Our national identity as Americans, and our federal identity as state citizens, are both represented in Congress—in the Senate and House."

Alas, the elements of the Constitution in which the elements of federalism are best exemplified—such as the Electoral College, the appointment of Senators by states, and the utilization of the 10th Amendment for the purposes of nullification—have been minimized by amendment, precedent, and political mission drift. Nevertheless, remnants of the old federalism remain, and they remain as bulwarks against tyranny.

ABOUT THE AUTHOR

George Grant is the Pastor of Parish Presbyterian Church, Director of the King's Meadow Study Center, Founder of both Franklin Classical School and New College Franklin, and Coordinator of the Chalmers Fund. He is the author of dozens of books in the areas of history, biography, politics, literature, and social criticism. He has pioneered efforts to establish Classical Christian Schools in the US and around the world. He makes his home in Middle Tennessee near the historic town of Franklin with his wife and co-author Karen. Together they have three grown children and six grandchildren. His essays, blogs, sermons, lectures, podcasts, and books may be found at GeorgeGrant.net.

Made in the USA
Middletown, DE
07 March 2025

72203835R00180